The 2004

PRUNE Book

The 2004 PRUNE Book

TOP MANAGEMENT CHALLENGES FOR PRESIDENTIAL APPOINTEES

JOHN H. TRATTNER
with Patricia McGinnis

COUNCIL FOR EXCELLENCE IN GOVERNMENT

BROOKINGS INSTITUTION PRESS
Washington, D.C.

About Brookings

The Brookings Institution is a private nonprofit organization devoted to research, education, and publication on important issues of domestic and foreign policy. Its principal purpose is to bring knowledge to bear on current and emerging policy problems. The Institution maintains a position of neutrality on issues of public policy. Interpretations or conclusions in Brookings publications should be understood to be solely those of the authors.

Library of Congress Cataloging-in-Publication data

Trattner, John H.
The 2004 prune book : top management challenges for presidential appointees / John H. Trattner with Patricia McGinnis, Council for Excellence in Government.
p. cm.
Summary: "A toolkit for incoming senior federal appointees, detailing the management dimensions of their jobs and explaining the underlying coordinating strategies that reflect current management practice in the federal government and its drive to improve performance, seen as the return on taxpayer dollars"—Provided by publisher.
Includes bibliographical references and index.
ISBN 0-8157-8327-2 (pbk. : alk. paper)
1. Government executives—United States. I. Title: Prune book. II. McGinnis, Patricia, CEO. III. Center for Excellence in Government (Washington, D.C.) IV. Title.

JK723.E9T7154 2005
352.2'93—dc22 2004024393

8 7 6 5 4 3 2 1

The paper used in this publication meets minimum requirements of the American National Standard for Information Sciences—Permanence of Paper for Printed Library Materials: ANSI Z39.48-1992.

Typeset in Sabon

Composition and design by Circle Graphics
Columbia, Maryland

Printed by R.R. Donnelley
Harrisonburg, Virginia

To honor the accomplishments of

Elliot L. Richardson

Longtime trustee, Council for Excellence in Government
Superb manager, unmatched achiever in public service,
perceptive and visionary leader

Contents

Acknowledgments

First mention here belongs to former Council Chair Frank A. Weil. As in the past, he stepped up to the challenge of funding the Prune Book in 2004 with vigor. A founding member of the Council and of the Prune project, Frank added to his very generous personal gift a strong, successful effort to develop support from other sources. Once again, the Council gratefully recognizes his financial support and leadership not only across seventeen years of Prune Book history, but also in his sturdy backing of other Council programs.

Our deep appreciation in this respect goes also to the Fannie Mae Foundation and the Touchstone Consulting Group, Inc., each a corporate partner of the Council. Franklin Raines, chair and chief executive officer of Fannie Mae—the Federal National Mortgage Association—took a personal role in the foundation's substantial grant toward the cost of Prune Book 2004's editorial production. Chris McGoff, Touchstone's chairman and chief executive officer, and Steve Lynott, president and chief operating officer, led their company's decision to help cover the cost of distributing the book to hundreds of leaders in the executive branch and the Congress. The contributions of all three, and of their organizations, were indispensable in producing the book and getting it into the hands of its key audience.

Mark Novitch, who robustly supported earlier volumes in this series, deserves our warm thanks for a further liberal and timely gift this year. His proactive interest and readiness to help have been significant factors in the achievements of the Prune Book series. We equally acknowledge the generous assistance of Harry Freeman, who secured a grant from the American Express Foundation to match his own gift. Harry was also the driving force behind the 1989 publication of our *Survivor's Guide for Government Executives*. Mark and Harry, both longtime Principals of the Council, typify the sustaining spirit and public-mindedness of the Council's membership.

Patricia McGinnis, the Council's president and chief executive officer, has had an important hand in the last three Prune Books, from conceptual vision to practical guidance. This time, she contributes a chapter as well. Thanks go to her for that and for her insightful participation, in a broad range of activities, in this year's book. She and I especially appreciate the work of Barry White, the Council's director of government performance projects, whose expertise, counsel, and drafting skill were vital in helping put the book together. We acknowledge his efforts here, in gratitude.

The Council greatly prizes the interest and energy given by current and past presidential appointees to the individual interviews we conducted as part of the research for the book. In senior public office, it is never easy to find time for such endeavors, however worthy the cause; those who did rendered a valuable service. For similar reasons, we are equally indebted to Council Principals who responded thoughtfully to the mini-interview to which we subjected them in an electronic survey. People who have served in appointed government posts constitute a singular resource for their immediate and later successors. We are fortunate to be able to tap it.

I want especially to thank Judith E. Michaels, who conducted all of the interviews for this book. Having studied, interviewed, and written about the political appointments process, she is no stranger to the issues addressed by Prune Books. To her interviewing assignment, Judith brought the experience and knowledge the job calls for and performed it with skill and stamina. The Council appreciates her work.

At the Council, Dan Paepke supplied solid administrative support to production of the book. A crucial element of that work was the daunting task of setting up interview appointments, coordinating with the interviewer, and keeping the timetable going amid inevitable postponements and reschedulings. Natalie Noakes, executive assistant to the president of the Council, helped that process with her calm pursuit of some critical but hard-to-get interviews. Jan Verrey again skillfully transcribed all of the interviews. I am lastingly grateful to these three able, persistent colleagues.

Other Council staff members helped in a variety of ways—advice, design, technology, budget, and substance. They are Najia Aziz-Arsalayee, Deborah Both, Shuron Coleman, Roz Docktor, Carl Fillichio, Cheri

Griffin, Katherine Hansen, Melissa Hardin, Janice Johnson, Meng Lin, David McClure, David Roberts, Anthony Shelborne, David Sheldon, David Skaggs, and Paulson Tharapatla. Thanks to all of them, and to each of them.

This is the second successive volume in the Prune Book series that the Council has copublished with the Brookings Institution Press. Again it has been a successful and enjoyable collaboration, for which much of the credit goes to director Robert Faherty, acquisitions editor Christopher Kelaher, art coordinator Susan Woollen, editors Charles Dibble and Tanjani Jacobson, proofreader Vicki Chamlee and indexer Julia Petrakis. It is a true pleasure to work with—and thank—them.

Introduction

Presidential appointees spend much of their time as managers. This book speaks primarily to them on that subject. In particular, it is for those fresh to their jobs, to Washington, or to both—people newly facing ideas, goals, and issues already familiar in varying degrees to those who have worked in or with government. Among the heavy demands on their talents and skills will be one of the heaviest of all—government's urgent need for results.

It's true that, as a term, "results" has worn somewhat thin. Like most such words, it tends to lose meaning through overuse. But the concept the word conveys has not. The fact remains that the need for better results is a powerful imperative driving government today. What are the reasons? Foremost by far are today's major challenges to national survival and progress. Not just the security of the country, not just its relations with the world. Other tough perennial concerns continue to haunt the United States in the early twenty-first century. Heading this familiar list are health care, education, the economy, the budget and taxes, social services, the environment, and the optimal, ethical management of science and technology. In dealing with them, government, with the most resources and reach, must lead the way.

Then come the perceptions of Americans about government's ability to produce the results they want. Opinion polls over the last decade, including those of the Council for Excellence in Government, support a reasonable conclusion that the public retains a basic faith in the ability of a well-managed government to get such results. But what has been clear for some time is Americans' sense of disconnection from government, their doubts about its positive impact on their lives, and their low interest in participation or service in it. At the same time, Americans as taxpayers look for a satisfactory return on their investment.

Getting results rests on two foundations: informed policy and smart management. Policy design identifies the problem, describes its solution, and sets the strategy, priorities, and tasks. As underscored by many observers, however, including those profiled in earlier Prune Books, policy does not get far without the support of good management by people and systems. Good management means program outcomes pursued sensibly and logically, with an eye toward accountability and cost-effectiveness. That may excite some people less than policy. But it is the main element in the results formula. It's a formula that presidential appointees charged with reaching policy goals should understand and apply. Thus the focus of the present volume.

In the first of this book's chapters, Patricia McGinnis, the Council's president and chief executive officer, takes stock of the expanding array of strategies, practices, and leadership skills that now serve those who manage for results. This tool kit covers multiple areas—from strategic planning in all its elements, to performance-based budget and operations decisions, to creating partnerships and setting priorities. The chapter also focuses on a theme that has become traditional in Prune Books and related Council publications: how to survive and succeed in an appointed position. As always, the insights and advice it offers on this theme come from appointees we interviewed for this book and from some seventy-five members—Principals—of the Council, all previous appointees themselves, whom we surveyed in May 2004.

The book's second section looks at the concepts that drive the current approach to measurably improved results in the management of the federal government. These four chapters discuss the mandates and coordinating entities involved, the leadership positions in agencies that are responsible for managing the effort, and important procedural mechanisms that support the management process.

Finally, a chapter by former Council chair Frank Weil and John Trattner of the Council staff examines the comments of present and former political appointees and Council Principals who, in the survey mentioned above, were asked to assess the value of the Prune Books and suggest improvements.

Because the *2004 Prune Book*'s essential focus is on today's government-wide approach to improving management, it contains fewer detailed individual position profiles than its predecessors. Readers interested in the details of specific appointed positions can consult dozens of profiles in earlier Prune Books. Copies of the most recent volume, *The 2000 Prune Book: How to Succeed in Washington's Top Jobs*, can be purchased from the Council for Excellence in Government (www.excelgov.org) and the Brookings Institution (www.brookings.edu).

In addition to the survey of Council Principals, and following established Prune Book practice, we interviewed a number of individuals who have held senior federal positions, many of them presidential appointees, as a major part of the research for the book. Because the book's focus is on current federal management and management approaches, most of those individuals were current appointees, in office when we talked with them. All of those we interviewed had the opportunity to review material derived from their interviews. We believe this procedure contributes to the book's accuracy and strengthens its authority.

PART ONE

SURVIVAL AND SUCCESS IN WASHINGTON

CHAPTER 1

How to Succeed in Washington

Getting Results for the People You Serve

PATRICIA McGINNIS

Congratulations! You have just been appointed by the president to a top job in government. In years past, political appointments, widely envied and regarded with high respect, were often referred to as "plum jobs." To describe them as "prune" jobs, as we do in the Prune Books, may be more accurate. A prune, in our lexicon, is a plum seasoned by wisdom and experience, with a much thicker skin.

A thick skin is essential armament in the politically charged environment in which you will be working. Partisan politics can be brutal, especially in the fishbowl created by the media, but politicians or media commentators are not necessarily out to get you; the obstacles that you may encounter are seldom actually about you. For example, a "hold" on the Senate's vote to confirm a presidential nominee is usually motivated by opposition to a policy or action of the president or another member of the administration, or by an attempt to gain leverage over the president or the administration, and may have nothing to do with you or your qualifications for the job.

So, if it is not about you, what is this very special opportunity really about? The most important answer—the most important single piece of advice in this chapter, from which everything else flows—is that you are here to achieve important results for the people you serve. Who are they? Broadly speaking, the American public; but specifically, they are the people whose lives are directly affected by the work of your agency, your office, and you yourself. If that remains uppermost in your mind, and if you succeed in making a significant difference in the lives of your constituency, you will have gotten it all right.

Some appointees get sidetracked from achieving their critical priorities by the sheer volume of their in boxes and the requirements that others place on them. You will have to find a way to maintain a focus on getting a few important things done while you are in office, leaving your institution and your team better than you found them.

Elliot Richardson, a founder of the Council for Excellence in Government, talked about what it takes to succeed as a leader in government at the last Council board meeting he attended before his death on December 31, 1999. This great public servant, the only person ever to serve in four cabinet positions, defined two leadership qualities necessary for effective governance in the new century. The first is a sense of history: knowing as much as reasonably possible about the context, the players, the successes, and failures that precede you. The second quality, somewhat antithetical to the first, is imagination: the ability to look around corners, to see a better future and enlist the assistance of others in giving form to that vision.

Richardson, who is a role model and mentor to me and to many who have served in government, often wisely described public service as a public trust, to be carried out with integrity and unqualified devotion to the public interest. His concept of integrity went beyond simple adherence to government ethics rules to encompass the "consistent pursuit of the merits . . . a willingness to speak up, to argue, to question, and to criticize, readiness to invite ideas, encourage debate, and accept criticism."

Personal Qualities

In the context of a sense of history, imagination, and integrity, several other qualities will serve you well. Teamwork, humility, focus, patience, and a sense of humor are important assets in the management of large organizations; in the executive branch, where so many interests intersect and, too often, conflict, they are essential.

Teamwork

Lone rangers rarely succeed in Washington—certainly not for very long. To succeed, appointees must be good at building their teams, starting with their agencies' core career staff; they should work with their peers in other agencies, with the White House, with the Office of Management and Budget (OMB), with members of Congress and their staffs, with the media, and with the many interest groups and stakeholders that inform every significant federal enterprise. Some will support you from the outset. Some will tolerate you—or at least not oppose you. Others will be your adversaries. Your adversaries on today's issue might be your allies on tomorrow's. To succeed in your job, you have to work with all of these interests, alienate as few as possible, and forge alliances—or at least détente—with most.

» There is no single individual, with the exception of, perhaps, the president, who wields great power on his own. I think that's a hard lesson for secretaries and assistant secretaries to learn. Power in Washington is diffuse. One succeeds and survives by building coalitions. [Kerry Weems, principal deputy assistant secretary for budget, technology, and finance, Department of Health and Human Services, George W. Bush administration]

» Communicate, communicate, and communicate—most of it by listening! Listen to people at all levels in the agency, to constituents, to Congress, and to the White House. [Mortimer Downey, deputy secretary and chief operating officer, Department of Transportation, Clinton administration]

» Know the key players that you have to work with to get things done . . . then find out what motivates them so that you can build a working relationship that is effective. [Failing to do] this is the single biggest shortcoming of people coming from the private sector. [Colin Blaydon, deputy associate director, Office of Management and Budget, Nixon administration]

Humility

It can be hard to be humble when you have been asked by the president to play a leading role in the government of the United States. Unless you have already served in similar positions, much of what you will face in government will be new to you. You may have been a senior executive of a major company or led an important interest group or served in high-profile positions in Congress or academia; none of these automatically prepares you to succeed in government. As you form your opinions and plan your strategies, take pains to appreciate what you don't know, listen to your predecessors, ask questions of your staff, and listen to what they say.

You will be urged to start off strong, take quick action, and put your personal stamp on your agency and position. That approach can be important, given the traditionally short tenure of most appointees. But a little humility in the beginning, seeking advice, really listening, and thinking through a variety of perspectives can help you avoid some of the pitfalls awaiting you and will enable you to achieve the results that will benefit the constituencies you serve.

» It's important to keep in mind that we all work for the people, and that we need to be responsible and accountable to a variety of parties, not just the executive branch, but also Congress, the press, and the public. [David M. Walker, comptroller general of the United States, appointed by Clinton administration; also served in Reagan and George H. W. Bush administrations]

» Be a little humble. Know that sycophants are not acting in your best interests. You need some people around that are able to tell you bad news. Sometimes they are the most valuable people you have. [Wade Horn, assistant secretary for children and families, Department of Health and Human Services, George W. Bush administration]

Focus

History tells us that most executive branch appointees stay in their jobs for between eighteen and twenty-four months. That is not much time to make a difference or to have a lasting impact. You should identify early on the critical few things that can be done in a reasonable period of time and work with your team and your partners to do them. At the same time, you will need to advance the resolution of longer-term issues that you may not see to completion. That way, your successor will not have to start at zero, and the public will not have to wait years for results.

To energize your team, work with them to articulate a compelling vision of the results you want to achieve and establish an ambitious time frame. If they are motivated to play a role in shaping your strategy, you will be in a strong position to reach out to build ownership and support. The urgency of a crisis causes people to focus and to act in ways that can be productive; in the absence of a crisis, you will have to create a sense of urgency the old-fashioned way—with good ideas, teamwork, and insistence on results.

» First, name three things you want to accomplish—and never lose focus on those. You want to "do" the job, not "be" the position. [Jack Ebeler, deputy assistant secretary, Department of Health and Human Services, Clinton administration]

» Crucial actions for appointees include a few compelling goals and aims that will energize the agency for a two- to four-year period, hopefully consistent with the stated goals of the administration and the constituencies. [Gil Omenn, associate director, Office of Management and Budget, Carter administration]

» Pick a few doable items and win on them. [Frank Hodsoll, deputy director for management, Office of Management and Budget, George H. W. Bush administration]

Patience

It may sound paradoxical, but as you focus on achieving a few really important results in a short time, you also have to be patient. Your willingness to listen, to learn, to compromise—even to abandon something on your shortlist or to add a new goal, if the opportunity arises and moves your vision forward—will require patience and perseverance. Many strategies can help you define these choices: consult your predecessors, consult your mentors, consult your allies in the administration, and consult your senior staff. But in the end, leadership carries with it the responsibility to act decisively and deliberately—when the time is right.

» In dealing with the big challenges in government, in addition to having positive leadership attributes and strong integrity, it often takes patience, then persistence, then perseverance, then pain, before you prevail. [David M. Walker, comptroller general of the United States]

» Don't let the plague of "in-box priorities" cause you to lose sight of the long-term strategy, but do identify every opportunity to link the two together. [Ruth A. David, deputy director for science and technology, Central Intelligence Agency, Clinton administration]

» If you're making a little progress day after day, you're going to change things. Whereas if you expect to shoot for the moon in a six-month or a year period, more than likely it ain't going to happen. And you end up with nothing. [David Safavian, administrator for federal procurement policy, Office of Management and Budget, George W. Bush administration]

A Sense of Humor

A good sense of humor is a terrific way to preserve your sense of self. Willard Wirtz, President Kennedy's secretary of labor, would often tell the story of visiting an elementary school during his tenure. A young girl came up to him and said: "I'm the labor secretary of the fourth grade!"

"That's wonderful! But what exactly does the labor secretary of the fourth grade do?" Wirtz asked.

With great pride, the girl said that she washed the blackboard and clapped the erasers at the end of the day; on Friday, she cleaned up all the mess so that everything was in place to start fresh on Monday. And then she inquired: "What exactly do *you* do?"

Without missing a beat, Wirtz replied: "Pretty much the same."

Washington is a place where the most serious business imaginable, the people's business, goes on every day. Humor is all too rare, but you will find that an appreciation of the occasional absurdities that you will encounter and have to deal with can go a long way in making your hard work and long hours more enjoyable. Think, for example, of what many appointees endure in the appointment and clearance process. A member of the Council for Excellence in Government described an incident that occurred before the formal Senate committee hearing on his confirmation:

» I was one of several nominees called to talk to members of the committee privately. I went in, and there was some back-and-forth around the table between them and me, the usual thing. I thought it was about over when Senator _____ came in. He plowed around in my record awhile and then said, "Now, I'd like to ask you about this vicious eight-page attack on the Congress of the United States that you authored and was reported in _____. What do you have to say about that?" I said, "Senator, I haven't the slightest idea what you're talking about." And then one of his staff leaned over to him and whispered, "Senator, it's not this guy, it's the next one." [*A Survivor's Guide for Government Executives* (Council for Excellence in Government, 1989)]

You will often encounter bureaucratic confusion and you will run into that kind of amusing absurdity. A light touch, when appropriate, will make your time in office more enjoyable and much more productive. Most of the people you deal with will value an even temper and a congenial manner and work all the better with you for it.

» The first thing to do is to have fun, enjoy what you do, and not get eaten up with your own sense of importance. You are only going to be there for a relatively short time, and when you leave, people are going to have to struggle to remember what the heck your name was. [Michael Jackson, deputy secretary of transportation, George W. Bush administration]

Combine these many qualities—a sense of history, imagination, integrity, teamwork, humility, focus, patience, and a sense of humor—to think and act strategically, with a view toward achieving results that will have a positive impact on the people you serve.

Resources and Tools You Need to Succeed

Although the personal qualities described above are indispensable, you will also need to make good use of a range of resources, tangible and intangible, to get results. Many come to Washington believing that civil servants, the budget process, information technology, other agencies, even the White House are forces to be tamed and managed. The reality is contrary: these are resources, and appointees need to use them skillfully and sensitively.

The People in Your Organization

Most civil servants have served or will serve in the executive branch longer than you; most are as committed as you are to achieving results for the American people. Political appointees typically devote a short time—eight years at the most—to government service. Civil servants, in contrast, are devoting their entire careers to the government; they have seen appointees come and go.

» As a political coming into the executive branch, people warned me about the civil service: "You can't trust them; they're always looking to push their own agenda rather than the president's agenda; be very cautious, watch what you say." The first bit of advice I would give is that the career folks, by and large, especially in the upper executive end, want to help you implement your agenda. They're there to help. They are not there to interfere. And you have to give them the benefit of the doubt. If you trust them and you build that trust in a relationship with them, you can get things done. [David Safavian, administrator for federal procurement policy, George W. Bush administration]

» You will find real talent among foreign service officers and career civil servants—use and respect them. [Hattie Babbitt, deputy administrator, United States Agency for International Development, Clinton administration]

The best civil servants welcome new leaders who bring new ideas, ask good questions, learn the ropes, and are committed to achieving results and strengthening the institution. Look for these people early, especially among the senior executives who report to you or your appointees. Heed their advice when you can; recognize, develop, and promote the best. One way to energize people, especially senior executives, is to offer and encourage mobility, within your agency or across agencies. Mobility broadens management perspectives.

Forging alliances with career staff becomes all the more important in light of the large turnover expected to occur in the civil service over the next few years, especially among senior executives. By 2008, according to the Office of Personnel Management, 52 percent of the current federal civilian workforce and 69.5 percent of all supervisors will be eligible to retire. Roughly 70 percent of all members of the senior executive service will be eligible to retire by 2008.

Cabinet heads may preside over scores of appointees. Subcabinet officials also oversee many appointees, and senior appointees not subject to Senate confirmation often supervise appointed staff. While subordinate appointees are, on paper, accountable to you, they often have their own lines of communication to the White House, Congress, and interest groups—and their own ideas.

You should be the leader of your entire workforce, both career and appointed, and get the best ideas and best work out of everyone, as a team.

Partnerships

In addition to working well with the people in your organization, partnerships with other federal agencies, state and local government agencies, the private sector, and nonprofit organizations will add immeasurably to your impact as a manager. Cultivate your partners, including new ones, strategically. Define the terms of the partnership, not only according to the rules (legal, regulatory, and contractual) but also to increase accountability for specific results.

Be creative about incentives and sharing experience to improve the process of partnerships. Use information technology wisely. For example, consolidating the application process for grants to state and local government has eliminated much redundancy; maybe that can be taken a step further in your area. Some agencies have used share-in-savings contracts with business partners to improve results and share financial risks. (Under a share-in-savings contract, a vendor pays for developing a product or service for an agency and is compensated from the savings it generates for that agency.) One such agency, the Department of Education, used that procedure to reengineer the management of student financial assistance.

» I always thought our best work was done in partnerships—among offices and agencies—with private and nonprofit organizations, with the Hill: better ideas, less friction, more efficient, better chance of mustering the resources and momentum to act. [Jamienne Studley, general counsel (acting), Department of Education, Clinton administration]

White House Staff

Each White House has its own personality, which reflects the leadership style of the president and his top advisers. Know who the players are, what roles they play, how decisions are made, and what is expected of you and your team. The president's chief of staff manages the White House staff and is usually very close to the president, from whom the power flows.

At times, you may get conflicting requests from various White House offices; in a fast-moving environment, coordination is not always perfect. The Office of Cabinet Affairs is usually the main liaison to cabinet agencies, but you may also deal with one of the policy shops or councils, such as the National Security Council or National Economic Council. Whatever the structures, know them, know the players, and know the president's agenda, especially in your area. And do not be surprised if the White House chooses to communicate good news coming from your agency and leaves you to communicate the bad news. You are part of the team.

» Know always that you are there to serve the president and the secretary—and that they are served by wisdom, candor, and loyalty, not blind obedience. [Jamienne Studley, general counsel (acting), Department of Education, Clinton administration]

Information Technology

The rapid advance of information technology, for good or ill, is a fact of life in any complex public or private organization. In the federal government, the advantages are enormous. Information and communications technology can gather, organize, integrate, and permit analysis of essential information from your staff, your grantees, and your contractors. It supports your financial management processes and enables you to learn quickly how well your agency is performing and what problems need to be solved. It provides ways for you to communicate with your colleagues, your partners, and the public. It can increase your agency's efficiency and reduce your costs, freeing resources for other priorities.

In the charge toward electronic government transactions and services, it is important to stay sharply focused on the citizens and businesses who are both the customers and owners of government. Public and private sector organizations often tend to approach service delivery from the inside looking out. Active engagement between government and citizens requires the contrary: understanding, identifying, and aligning the government's actions with the priorities of the people being served. The customer occupies the center of the e-government revolution. The next phase of e-government development should focus on breakthrough performance, solving problems, and achieving tangible results. The "gold standard" measures of e-government's performance must include the following, each of which should be measured regularly:

—Improvements in *quality:* delivering reliable, accurate, and user-friendly information, transactions, and services; and integrating them across government agencies and levels of government, using commercial best practices. Customer satisfaction is the key index here.

—Improvements in *cycle time:* delivering information and services in minutes or seconds, not hours, days, weeks, or months. Efficient e-government reduces processing time for transactions, information requests, decisions, and problem resolution.

—*Cost* reductions: raising efficiencies in average and per-unit service delivery costs for government activities and transactions; information technology can avoid duplicative submission of data.

Of course, technology alone is not the final answer. Achieving higher levels of government performance must also involve motivating people and improving processes. Success in government is conditioned on all of these factors.

If you are coming into government as a chief information officer, these guidelines will probably be familiar. If you will be heading an agency, you should get close to your chief information officer. Take the time to investigate how your goals can be advanced through the strategic, creative use of technology.

The Budget

Virtually all significant public policy initiatives require funding. Decisions about the level of public resources you will get for your initiatives are made in your agency's internal budget process, in the coordination among agencies of the president's budget proposal to Congress, and in the congressional budget, appropriation, and authorization processes. The resources you want will rarely come to you unless you make significant efforts to influence each of these processes. You must know the players, know the schedule, and know when and how to get involved.

Your staff will include budget experts, notably a career budget officer and program managers. These people understand the mechanics of the budget and have been through it many times. If you are a component of a larger department, you will find more key budget players at the department level, both career budget officers and appointees. The program associate director, or PAD, within the Office of Management and Budget who has jurisdiction over your area will have considerable influence in the formulation of your budget. Each program associate director has a career division chief (the head of a resource management office), a branch chief, and examiners who review your programs and your management. These career people have extraordinary influence on the success of your proposals. In Congress, appropriations and authorization committee members and staff have authority to influence and approve your budget. Sometimes a junior committee member will be your key contact. If yours is an "orphan" agency, the sponsorship of a junior member or subcommittee staff can make a large difference in your agency's appropriation. Senators and representatives outside the committees, as well as their aides, may have an interest in decisions affecting your programs. And many interest groups with a stake in your budget issues can be as important as any of the government officers or legislators involved.

This is a very long list, but each person on it has the ability to make your success more or less likely. You should know what each of these players thinks is important and discuss your ideas with them.

For your strategies to succeed, you have to play a lead role in each of the budget decisionmaking and negotiation processes. Modulate your positions to reflect what has worked in the past and to agree with the president's goals (which you help shape). Take into account the frequently conflicting views of Congress and the interest groups. Work out a strategy for getting proposals through each process. All this takes time and effort, but it is worth it in the end.

The schedules for budgeting can involve three different fiscal year budgets at the same time: (1) the budget funding your current activity; (2) the budget pending in Congress for the current or next fiscal year; and (3) the budget being developed for the president's budget for the year following. Specific schedules change every year, but your intervention can be decisive at several key points:

—The budget that funds current activity does not run on autopilot. You have to take an active interest in how your programs are working or you may miss a key moment to intervene. You have to be the first to recognize and respond to a problem. If OMB, the Government Accountability Office (GAO), Congress, interest groups, or the media get wind of problems, you will spend valuable time putting out fires instead of getting the best out of your budget resources.

—Once the president's budget goes to Congress, it becomes the pending budget. Both the House and the Senate may schedule multiple hearings on your budget, always before appropriations subcommittees, sometimes before the budget committees, and often before authorizing committees in whose jurisdictional area of the budget you and/or they are proposing changes. Appointees are the usual witnesses, though sometimes career budget officers and program managers also testify. The career officers are in frequent contact with the staff, providing you with key intelligence and helping build support. The congressional process is supposed to end in late spring with enactment of appropriations bills, but negotiations may extend up to—and sometimes well beyond—the end of the fiscal year.

These tasks are difficult—and nearly impossible to do well—your first time around, but your first budget may be the most important. You can get help. Learn from your career staff, from experienced predecessors and allies in the administration and Congress, and from sympathetic interest groups.

—Formulation of the budget for the following year starts in the spring with your ideas. You will have some general guidance from OMB on funding levels for your agency or division. They may not be binding, but most appointees oversee multiple programs and staffs, so here is where compromise and accommodation begin. The justification to OMB is developed in the summer—on your own if you head an independent agency or blended with your peers' inputs (where more compromises will occur) if you are in a department. Proposals are submitted to OMB in September.

You may be called to testify at OMB staff hearings in the fall or to respond to written questions. Seize every opportunity to make your case with OMB. Unless you get everything you ask for in initial decisions ("the OMB pass-back")—a virtually unheard-of event—in late fall and early winter you make your case in appeals or seek support from White House aides to influence OMB. For the very biggest issues, you may get to present your case to the chief of staff and other advisers or even to the president in December and January. The budget goes to Congress in February. Before that, you formally or informally brief Congress, the media, and interest groups to gauge support or opposition, perhaps modifying your proposals in response.

» Nothing actually gets done unless resources are provided in the budget. [Joseph Kasputys, assistant secretary of commerce, Ford administration]

Congress

"The president proposes, and Congress disposes," so the saying goes. That fundamental principle is set out in the Constitution. And the fact that it is Article I of the Constitution that established Congress and its powers reflects the founders' views of the importance of the legislative branch.

In reality, power has shifted markedly toward the executive branch over the history of the republic, a trend that accelerated with the New Deal, World War II, and the cold war. Nonetheless, few executive branch appointees can be effective without remaining mindful of the role of Congress, its committees, and its key members. The power of the purse and the leverage that Congress has in controlling annual appropriations are a fact of life for every department and agency.

The interaction between the executive and the legislative branch is intricate and convoluted. While not all appointees work directly with Congress, you should learn as much as you can about the committees and the members (of both parties) who will have a major say in your agency's funding and functions.

In addition to the budget, several types of concrete tasks related to Congress await you and your staff. These may include formulating legislative initiatives for the administration; drafting bills, amendments, and explanatory material (often called "report language") on behalf of these initiatives' House and Senate sponsors; writing testimony for congressional hearings; and of course, responding to congressional inquiries or investigations. You may work with interest groups to form coalitions before formal legislation surfaces. You will test public reactions to legislative ideas, sometimes following public opinion, sometimes challenging it. You will consult and work closely with your allies in Congress, but also with your adversaries. You will develop long-term and temporary alliances, depending on the issue; remember always that your opponent in a current policy debate may be your partner next time.

Get to know your congressional liaison and others in your agency's governmental affairs department. Both career and political staff in these departments know the often mysterious and opaque ways of Capitol Hill. Learn from them. Listen to them. Most important, work with them.

Many on the Hill—some even in your party—may disagree with much that you believe. But you must always respect the constitutional roles they have to play, as you hope they will respect yours. Remember that the checks and balances framed in the Constitution were designed to make policy change a cumbersome business.

» Success in Washington is all about relationships within your shop and with those in other areas with whose work or impact you intersect. It is also about understanding the constitutional assignment of equal roles for the executive and congressional branches. Forget this at your peril. [Bill Brock, secretary of labor, Reagan administration]

» Pay attention to Congress, but do what is right (even if it is politically unpopular). [Jacques Gansler, under secretary of defense for acquisition, technology, and logistics, Clinton administration]

» Don't neglect Congress—that is the usual failing of people coming from outside Washington to take a senior position. In the end, Congress decides your budget and may decide your programs. Go visit and make good links. [D. James Baker, under secretary of commerce for oceans and atmosphere, Clinton administration]

» Be honest with people on the Hill. They understand that you can't always be forthcoming, but that's no excuse for being misleading.

> And remember that some of the senior career people in your shop probably have well-established relationships with congressional staff and members that can work for you. Or, if you're not careful, against you. [Rep. David Skaggs (D-Colo.), 1987–99]

The Media

Whether we like it or not, the media have become our modern-day civics teachers. With the advent of twenty-four-hour cable news, the resurgence of talk radio, aggressive marketing and competition among newspapers and weekly magazines, and the explosive growth of the Internet, American news media are by far the most influential voices in bringing ordinary citizens information—and shaping their opinions—about government.

The question for you is simple: do you want the media to work in partnership with you or work against you? The answer is easy; the reality is not. Media coverage of the federal government is changing—and not for the better.

According to a 2003 study conducted for the Council for Excellence in Government by the Center for Media and Public Affairs, there is far less coverage of the federal government than there used to be on evening network broadcasts, as well as on the front pages of national and regional newspapers. Reporting on the federal government is increasingly judgmental, opinionated, and generally negative. The average "news hole" on network television broadcasts—after subtracting time for commercials and promotions from the half-hour time slot—decreased from 22 minutes, 22 seconds in 1981 to 18 minutes, 37 seconds by 2001. It is probably even shorter today.

Despite these discouraging statistics, it is still possible—and even more imperative—to tell your story to the American people through the media. Network television is not the only outlet: local news channels, cable, print, Internet, and other media are powerful. Your agency and its programs are probably covered by specialized newsletters and Washington bureaus. Get to know their reporters and editors. Building relationships will be essential to your success. Your agency's public affairs office (the "press shop") is the first step; a good working relationship with the career and political staff in the press office is vital. Don't delay your first encounter with these professionals until a media crisis looms. Take the time to get to know them, and give them an early opportunity to get to know you and your programs. Include them when you begin developing policy, and listen carefully to their suggestions. Having a communications component at the start of a project will prevent missteps when the project is announced or implemented. The public affairs staff usually has its ear to the ground with reporters who are interested in your programs. That intelligence can be immensely helpful to you.

Cultivate relationships—and two-way trust—with the media: reporters from trade publications, beat reporters at major newspapers, cable and network producers and correspondents, and content managers and writers on news websites. Learn to understand their needs and how their game is played. Treat them as equals. Relationships built through trust will serve you well.

What role can you play in helping to reverse these trends? You need to ask yourself some key questions: How can I work more effectively with journalists to foster credible and understandable reporting of complex government issues? How can I use both my expertise and credibility as a government news source to achieve better results not just for reporters, but also for my agency and the people I serve?

» Officials need to recognize that the people have a right to know what public officials are doing with their authorities, and with the people's money. They need to be responsive to the media and the public. At the same time, we all recognize that the media isn't always going to get it right. And that's life. But it's better to be responsive. It's better to be honest and open than the opposite. [David M. Walker, comptroller general of the United States]

The Public

Public service is a public trust: the people are sometimes your customers, but they are always your ultimate overseers, as the owners of our democracy.

Many leaders in government see the public as distant and not sufficiently informed to be involved in the substance of their work. To be sure, most people will not know much about you or your job, but they know what their priorities are, what they will support or oppose, and whether the administration's policy and practice are relevant to them or their families. Just a few years ago, a Council for Excellence in Government poll found that a majority of Americans—especially young Americans—no longer think of government as "of, by, and for the people." For them, it is "the" government, not "our" government. The September 11, 2001, attacks changed that temporarily, but the long-term health of our democracy and the vitality of our government depend on greater participation by citizens, not only voting but also helping set priorities and holding government accountable for results.

You can communicate with the public in a number of ways: indirectly, by working with their elected representatives, or directly, in town hall meetings or online. For example, in 2003 the Council for Excellence in Government held a series of town hall meetings around the country to look at homeland security from the citizens' perspective. These conversations, reinforced by expert working groups and national polls, led to tangible changes in policy and practice among the federal, state, and local leaders who participated. Trust the people: they have a lot to offer to help you in responding to their needs.

» I think some people who are having their first run in a senior government job will be surprised at how much time they spend thinking about how to communicate effectively with the public and making sure they do so. [Michael Jackson, deputy secretary of transportation, George W. Bush administration]

Use these resources—build your team; create partnerships; listen and work closely with the White House, Congress, and the media; do your homework; and engage the public in setting your agenda. Choose a few critical priorities, with clearly aligned goals and measures, for individuals, teams, partners, and your agency. Measure performance and communicate progress and results honestly to your team, your partners, Congress, the media, and the public. This will go a long way to building your credibility and restoring trust in government, which you should regard as part of your job.

Effective Leadership

Government boils down to effective leadership, about which much has been written and said. President Harry Truman, who usually got right to the heart of things in a very few words, once said that a leader is "someone who can get other people to do what they don't want to do and like it."

What does it take to be a leader? John Gardner, a legendary public sector leader who founded Common Cause and won the Presidential Medal of Freedom, cautioned that leadership is not to be confused, as it often is in Washington, with status, power, or official authority. Instead, effective leadership focuses on vision, values, crossing boundaries, thinking into the future, constant renewal, and inspiring and raising trust.

What do leaders do? Gardner said that leaders define what the future should look like, align people to that vision, and inspire them to make it happen despite the obstacles. Management expert Peter Drucker says that popularity is not leadership: "Leadership is all about achieving results for the people you serve. Effective leaders in government are collaborative, smart, and accountable for results." In a public survey on attitudes about government leaders conducted by Peter Hart and Bob Teeter for the Council for Excellence in Government in 1997, nearly two-thirds of the respondents said that politicians who pursue their own rather than the public's agenda are a major cause of reduced confidence in government. Very few respondents said that leaders spend tax dollars wisely (13 percent), tell the truth (14 percent), put politics aside to do what is right (15 percent), or understand average people (20 percent).

To provide context, public trust in the federal government "to do what is right just about always or most of the time" (a formulation frequently used in polls) has declined substantially over the last forty years—from a high of 76 percent in 1964 to 36 percent in 2003, according to a series of University of Michigan surveys conducted since 1958. Public trust in government dropped from 53 percent to 36 percent between 1972 and 1974 (Watergate), increased from 33 percent to 44 percent between 1982 and 1984 (Ronald Reagan's first term), increased from 27 percent to 40 percent between 1996 and 1998 (Bill Clinton's second term), increased to 56 percent after September 11, 2001, and then declined to 36 percent in 2003, the level at which it stood in 1974.

You have a role in building trust in government. Improving the performance of your institution matters to the American people.

» Set high standards for performance for yourself and those with whom you work. [Joseph Kasputys, assistant secretary of commerce, Ford administration]

» Focus on aligning resource decisions with results. [Mark Forman, administrator, office of e-government and information technology, Office of Management and Budget, George W. Bush administration]

» It is important to measure performance, because what gets measured gets improved. [Josh Gotbaum, executive associate director and controller, Office of Management and Budget, Clinton administration]

» Getting the team committed to meaningfully quantified goals is crucial. [Charles Rossotti, commissioner of internal revenue, Clinton and George W. Bush administrations]

» It's not about how hard you try; it's about the results you achieve. [David Safavian, administrator for federal procurement policy, George W. Bush administration]

Three striking examples show how visionary leadership coupled with clearly defined goals, team building, and performance accountability can produce extraordinary results. One is the turnaround in the 1990s of the Federal Emergency Management Agency (FEMA), now a part of the Department of Homeland Security. Plagued by its belief that it was statutorily unauthorized to act in emergencies until state governments asked it to, FEMA had been spending most of its budget on a program to maintain communications for government leaders after a nuclear attack—well after the end of the cold war. FEMA struggled under the oversight of twenty congressional committees. One representative proposed eliminating the agency altogether.

Taking over as director in 1993, James Lee Witt focused the agency's major departments on its most important responsibilities. He appointed a team of senior career managers to revamp FEMA's mission and develop a reorganization plan. He sought employee comments on what needed fixing. He discussed the reorganization with the chairs of the twenty oversight committees. FEMA was soon actively engaged in disaster response, positioning resources before disasters struck, and nourishing rebuilt relationships with state agencies. Resources previously earmarked for nuclear attack went to hurricane preparedness and other realities. The agency used technology and better communications to improve customer service. Every senior executive changed jobs within the agency. As a result, the House bill to abolish FEMA was withdrawn, and Witt and FEMA employees were commended for dramatic improvements in the agency's performance. State disaster relief officials were also pleased. And in opinion surveys, more than 80 percent of respondents rated the agency's service good to excellent.

One of the points this success story makes is that innovative leaders are not content merely to respond. They look for opportunities to pursue critical priorities, engage their senior career leaders, seek innovative partnerships, and communicate effectively with Congress and the public.

A second example is the response of the Food and Drug Administration (FDA) to long-standing criticism of the slow pace of its drug approval process. Tasked with evaluating the safety and effectiveness of new drugs and medical products before they are marketed, the FDA is known as the gold standard for review; many other countries rely on its judgments. But drug manufacturers, who spend huge sums to develop their products, complained that long delays in approval delayed sales. Patient advocates complained that delays in new drug approvals denied important treatments to people with serious diseases and argued that faster approvals would ease or prevent suffering and reduce mortality.

An agreement between Congress, drug manufacturers, and the FDA produced the Prescription Drug User Fee Act, which authorized the agency to charge manufacturers scaled fees for its drug reviews in return for accelerating the approval process. These actions also generated significant operational and cultural change within the FDA's Center for Drug Evaluation and Research. Using performance evaluation, project management, and peer review mechanisms, the center's leadership made its staff accountable for meeting the targets of the new legislation. By 1997, new drug applications had risen by 45 percent, while the median period for review and approval had fallen from twenty-two months to six for drugs in the priority category and to twelve months for less urgent new drugs. Better communication between manufacturers and FDA staff has produced better-prepared applications. The drug fee legislation was renewed in 1997 for another five years, with tougher review goals and authority for innovations to further speed the review process and the development of new drugs. A senior civil servant led this turnaround: Janet Woodcock, director of the FDA's Center for Drug Evaluation and Research.

The final example is the success of the Transportation Security Administration (TSA) in meeting the exceptional demands generated by the events of September 11. The TSA was born of those terrorist attacks, built under heavy pressure, and intended from the beginning to form part of another new and larger agency. Simultaneously, it faced short deadlines for daunting and unprecedented safety tasks—most important, federalizing and improving security at U.S. airports. This was a start-up story unequaled in the federal government since World War II.

Congress created the TSA on November 19, 2001, and set a one-year deadline for the agency to deploy and train the federal security workforce in all 429 U.S. commercial airports. Ten months later, the agency had hired 32,000 screeners, stationed them at nearly a hundred airports, and assigned 145 federal security directors and deputy directors to manage security at 380 airports. At the one-year deadline, the TSA had screeners working at all 429 airports and was screening all checked baggage. The agency called it the largest peacetime mobilization in the country's history.

Since then, the TSA has continued to improve airport security. In May 2004, the agency issued security guidelines for general aviation (noncommercial) airports, with federally endorsed security enhancements and methods for implementation and a measurement process that helps define each airport's unique security needs. The tool enables airport administrators to evaluate an airport's security characteristics and decide optimal enhancements for their facilities. It covers the security needs of small, privately owned landing strips in rural areas as well as large commercial airports in major cities. The TSA story is one of collaboration, a strategic approach, unusual partnerships, and accountability for seemingly impossible results and deadlines.

As these three stories demonstrate, your appointment presents you with a great opportunity and grants you the privilege to serve. Despite their many war stories and tales of anguish, most of your predecessors—former appointees who are now in the private sector—say that their time in government was the most challenging, most rewarding experience of their careers: "the best job I ever had." We wish the same for you and for the people you serve.

PART TWO

FEDERAL MANAGEMENT TODAY

JOHN H. TRATTNER

CHAPTER 2

Results: Concept and Action

In the senior political positions of today's federal executive branch, achieving success—getting results—is arguably as tough as it has ever been. Difficult and demanding in themselves, many of the jobs steer through the tricky cross-currents of governance at a time when government faces an array of problems of rare complexity. That puts an extra premium on results: on getting a desired product for the time, effort, and money expended.

Desired results depend on far more than the funding invested in an attempt to produce them. But the public's money, and how well it is deployed through the federal budget, remains the central gear in the machine of government. Simply put, the budget process distributes federal resources among competing programs and priorities. Around it swirl the main questions of governance in general and management in particular. Which programs to pursue toward policy objectives? How much should be spent on them? What results should be expected, how should they be measured, and who is accountable if the results do not meet expectations? How best to engage the workforce? How can managers establish a meaningful, measurable connection between budget and performance so that future funding reflects proven results?

Over more than half a century, government has tried periodically to devise conclusive ways to answer such questions. This chapter and the three that follow go to the concept, approaches, and procedures through which today's federal executive is seeking those answers. These chapters are about how to link programs' performance and the money allocated to them. They are about more focused accountability, about the strengthened attempt at government-wide coordination of functions like financial and workforce management and the powerful resource offered by electronic government, and about the central mechanisms and agency positions engaged in trying to make it all happen.

A Little History

Repeated executive branch attempts since the mid-twentieth century to improve government efficiency had a common theme—results—but fell short when it came to implementation. None lasted long. Successive administrations came up with their own approaches, dating back at least to the Hoover Commission report under Presidents Harry Truman and Dwight Eisenhower. Later came Lyndon Johnson's Program-Planning-Budgeting System, Richard Nixon's Management by Objectives, Jimmy Carter's Zero-Based Budgeting, Ronald Reagan's Grace Commission, and Bill Clinton's National Performance Review.

In the early 1990s, a watershed: Congress moved directly to push management reform in the executive branch with passage of the Chief Financial Officers Act of 1990 (the CFO Act). Aimed at improving federal financial management and hailed by some as the most significant such legislation in forty years, the CFO Act established chief financial officers in the cabinet and major agencies. It created the job of deputy director for management at the Office of Management and Budget—OMB—and the post of controller heading OMB's Office of Federal Financial Management. And it strengthened the powers of those who would lead its implementation at OMB and in the agencies.

Looking back, however, the CFO Act's greater significance lay in setting the stage, especially on Capitol Hill, for developing the more expansive Government Performance and Results Act of 1993 (GPRA). GPRA called for the application of strategic planning covering each program activity set forth in agency budgets; annual public reporting on performance; improving resource allocation, program design, and program management decisions; and increasing the use of high-quality program evaluation—rigorous measurement of results against the funding invested.

While some of these directives echoed the intent of the earlier initiatives, GPRA was different. Like the CFO Act, its statutory basis made possible the continuity of its provisions across administrations. Both the executive branch and Congress could use the data it produces to make fairer, more efficient, more effective use of public financial resources. And GPRA presented an opportunity to compare achievements with goals, design better programs, manage them better, and give Americans a better chance to hold government accountable for the results they want.

But GPRA was by no means the final answer. During the first ten years following its enactment, implementation suffered from a lack of strong executive branch leadership. Responsibility for the GPRA process often lodged at lower levels of federal agencies, with no ties to budgeting, financial management, or human resources. Nor was there much evidence that Congress valued or was using GPRA's performance and results information in authorizing or funding programs. Serious gaps developed in the act's implementation, especially in connecting performance plans and reports to important management and budget decisions.

GPRA, however, did stir new thinking and altered some practices. Some federal agencies did raise the quality of their strategic planning and annual performance reports. Some did change the way they managed against performance goals. GPRA brought new attention to an old word—*performance;* to judging performance—*measurement;* and to performance's product—*results.* John Koskinen, OMB's deputy director for management in the Clinton administration, thought GPRA had "caused people to focus on what difference programs are making. And a big part of the answer to what difference we are making with a program is how well it is organized and managed." Gradually, in the late 1980s and especially during the 1990s, the effort to rationalize and improve federal management, boosted by such initiatives as the Clinton-era establishment of the President's Management Council, gained broader footing and wider acceptance.

The President's Management Agenda

In 2001, the launch of the President's Management Agenda—PMA—injected tangible vigor into this progression. The five-point agenda, says Clay Johnson, OMB's deputy director for management, "is really about the work that has to be done to make the federal government results-oriented." The federal government has 1,200 or 1,300 programs, on which it spends more than $2 trillion annually, Johnson points out.

» On a regular basis, we need to be asking ourselves if these programs are working. If not, what are we going to do about them? We are committed to doing everything possible to make sure that every program authorized by Congress, for which funds were appropriated, is working at the desired level. We should always be looking for ways to do it more effectively, more efficiently, to try

BOX 2-1. Focus of the President's Management Agenda

- Strategic management of human capital
- Competitive sourcing
- Improved financial performance
- Expanded electronic government
- Budget and performance integration

to get more good done for the amount of money we have. The PMA is about managing assets.

A "management scorecard" tracks the progress of departments and major agencies toward the goals of the five PMA initiatives (see box 2-1). It uses a simple traffic-light scheme to mark progress, in which green means success, yellow signals mixed results, and red flashes a message of unsatisfactory. "Most government agencies are not at the green light; they're at the red light or the yellow light," says David Walker, comptroller general of the United States, who heads the Government Accountability Office (the GAO, formerly the General Accounting Office), a congressional agency with watchdog functions over the executive branch.

» We're dealing with issues of long-standing concern. You don't solve long-standing problems overnight. But it's critically important that you have a priority list, that you be focused on it, and that you have mechanisms to provide a certain degree of transparency and accountability on whether or not people are making progress in the things that you care the most about. The stop-light approach has been a very effective approach.

The ongoing scorecard results for each individual organization, updated quarterly, are posted on a comprehensive, information-rich website: www.results.gov. Subtitled *Resources for the President's Team* and directed specifically at appointees, the site is meant as part tool kit, part cheerleader. It updates appointees and all senior federal executives about the pursuit of PMA goals and related objectives; gives them a variety of helpful facts, fundamentals, and tools; and presses them to move forward.

Here are some of Clay Johnson's comments on specific points of the PMA:

» *Financial management.* This is about cost management. Federal managers must have timely and accurate cost information to produce desired results at an acceptable cost. So agencies must be able to account for their financial activity to the point that they are able to get unqualified audit opinions and close their books within at least forty-five days of the end of the fiscal year. And then they must use this financial information on a regular basis to manage their costs. We help agencies establish the disciplines and management practices they need to proactively manage their costs.

» *Electronic government.* It manages service levels. Someone wants to look for a job. People want to inquire about benefits, about grants. Right now, it's a treasure hunt to look around and figure all this out. Let's come up with a single Internet portal you can go to that helps you navigate through the labyrinth of the federal government. It's to better serve people who want to know what benefits are due to them, what grants options they have, what jobs are available. E-government uses the technology to focus on what the needs of the citizen are, not what the capability of the agency is. It's using the technology across agency lines to deal with our citizens, as opposed to taking twenty-six different approaches to it.

» *Human capital.* We spend $110 billion a year on the civilian workforce, 1.8 million people, our most valuable asset. What are we doing to make sure that workforce always has clear direction, good management, key skills, is never lacking for people? If there are a lot of retirements, do we have plans in place to fill those retirements before they happen? If people are well trained, they're well motivated. There are lots of reasons to be attracted to employment here, to be highly motivated, to want to continue to work here. That's the human capital objective.

» *Competitive sourcing.* A fourth of our labor money, about $25 billion, is spent to do work that's really commercial. Is the best way to do that work—like printing or food service—to use federal employees? Let's figure out the best way to do it internally and the best way to do it externally with commercial staff, then figure out which of those is better for the taxpayer.

A word about competitive sourcing. Not new as a concept, it seeks to get the best product or service at the least cost by comparing alternate ways of producing it. In the context of the President's Management Agenda, it was applied to thousands of federal jobs to see if they could be better and more cheaply performed in the private sector. Even if the jobs ultimately remained in government, competing them against the private sector was meant to raise their efficiency.

But that approach proved contentious from the outset. Critics faulted competitive sourcing for its across-the-board sweep, which made it unlikely to register crucial distinctions between functions that can and cannot be performed better somewhere else. Nor, they said, did it take into account the difficulties in comparing the costs of public and private sector employment, which have very different health insurance, career track, retirement, and other features. In March 2004, the GAO reported that competitive sourcing had centered "more on targets and milestones for conducting competitions than on the outcomes the competitions are designed to produce: savings, innovation, and performance improvements."

Johnson acknowledges mistakes in the early going. "As agencies started moving along, we weren't focused enough on collecting and dealing with the facts," he says. "So we didn't have the database that we could refer to. We're changing that." David Safavian, a senior General Services Administration official who when we talked with him had been nominated as director of the Office of Federal Procurement Policy, described the competitive sourcing initiative as "very controversial, a horrid experience in terms of implementation." Nonetheless, he said that, of more than six hundred competitions in 2003, "federal employees won 89 percent of them" and kept those jobs in the hands of federal workers. "We spent about $90 million to bring competitive sourcing government-wide," Safavian added, "and saved the taxpayers—or avoided them some costs—totaling $1.1 billion net."

And budget and performance integration? In particular, this directive lends further definition and conviction to the idea that realistic, effective management of the budget requires genuine integration of budget and performance. Where GPRA execution failed to adequately tie goals, performance, and public reporting to critical budget decisions, the PMA makes the connection between dollars and results explicit and mandatory. Setting standards and rating performance, it also incorporates the Program Assessment Rating Tool—PART—which systematically arrays what is known about individual program design, management, and results.

PART is an analytical device developed for use by OMB and agency managers. Its disciplined, methodical organization of data contributes to budget and management decisionmaking in agencies and in the president's budget process. It does that by engaging agency and OMB staff in a focused, collaborative determination of what "the best available evidence" means. It gives agency managers a snapshot of each program, relatively free of advocacy. This allows an objective focus on management issues (federal, contractor, and grantee) and on program impact, a focus that relates to purpose. It surfaces program design flaws in legislation and in regulation. As the number of PART-ed programs grows, the process will for the first time permit systematic assessment of similar programs in multiple agencies.

"They've stated their intention to look at 100 percent of all major federal programs over a five-year period," says the GAO's Walker. He doesn't think PART is a panacea. "But it is a positive step. And the results are surprising, because a very significant percentage (of programs)—I think it's close to half—cannot demonstrate they are making a difference, on an outcome basis, with the resources, the authorities, and the people that they have invested. That is unacceptable." He therefore supports the time and attention engaged by PART and views with satisfaction the additional transparency he sees coming out of it.

"It's tempting in this business to create new initiatives and new programs that are not effectively measured and tested beforehand," says Asa Hutchinson, under secretary for border and transportation security at the Department of Homeland Security. "You get committed to them long term before you really have an opportunity to measure them. With the pressures of performance, it's easy to move forward aggressively without having those proper measuring sticks." For this reason, it is critical for managers "to hold those programs accountable in each budget cycle. You have to look back at what might be obsolete, what might have been rendered redundant because of new technologies and new systems that are in place, and not simply perpetuate the same programs and budgets year after year. You have to measure investments very carefully."

Thus does the budget and performance integration required by the President's Management Agenda give momentum, government-wide, to the principles evoked in GPRA. Comptroller General Walker made that clear when he reminded a House committee in September 2003 of a key GPRA objective: to help the executive branch and Congress better understand how results relate to outlays. "Linking planned performance with budget requests and financial reports," he said, "is an essential step in building a culture of performance management."

Speaking with us, Walker described most of the federal government as "an amalgamation of policies, programs, functions, and activities over a number of decades, which made sense when they were enacted into law but have not been subject to a fundamental review and reexamination since." Given the current budget deficit and projected fiscal situation, he says, "the base of government is not sustainable." Therefore, a "fundamental reexamination" of the proper role of the federal government in the twenty-first century is imperative. Such an assessment should ask what the government should do, how the government should do its business, in some cases who should do its business, and what kinds of results are being generated with the resources available. "Clearly, that's something that this administration is very focused on," Walker adds.

The GAO, he points out, "has been focused for some time on a number of major management challenges. And on areas that represent a higher risk of fraud, waste, abuse or mismanagement, and more recently on areas that are in need of a fundamental transformation, whether it's programs, government entities, or functional areas." A look at the GAO's high-risk list, he says, shows "a very strong correlation with the President's Management Agenda. That's no accident."

Elaborating, Walker says the GAO has worked closely with OMB in the last two administrations, both of which "have tended to be more interested in management issues, especially [the George W. Bush] administration." The goal of this particular interaction has been to exchange ideas on which areas need focus. "Through those ongoing dialogues the president and his representatives obviously have to make their own judgment about what their priorities are going to be," he says. But the fact of "two very important, prominent, and powerful institutions focusing on some of the same issues increases the likelihood that you're going to have positive and sustainable outcomes."

The President's Management Council

The President's Management Council—PMC—dates from 1993, when the Clinton administration designated the deputy secretary or another top official in each Cabinet department, and equivalent senior officials in other large agencies, as chief operating officers, or COOs. Comparable in some respects to their private sector opposite numbers, these twenty COOs functioned as the top managers of their agencies. At the same time, they retained their responsibilities in developing and executing policy and running their own organizations (see chapter 4). The COOs represented their agencies in the President's Management Council, created at the same time.

BOX 2-2. Functions of the President's Management Council

- Improve overall executive branch management, including PMA implementation
- Coordinate management-related efforts to improve government throughout the executive branch, resolving specific interagency management issues as necessary
- Ensure adoption of new management practices in the executive branch
- Identify, and provide for interagency exchange of, best management practices

Source: Presidential memorandum, announced in July 2001.

"People really liked coming to the meetings," says Edward DeSeve, deputy director for management at OMB from 1998 to 2001. "It was three hours a month out of their schedules—you couldn't send someone in your place—where they talked about issues they cared about and were causing them problems." To help fix such problems, the PMC might call on its own members with the relevant experience or bring in appropriate experts. It also put a number of issues on its agenda each year, such as workforce downsizing and GPRA implementation.

In 2001, the Bush administration renewed the President's Management Council as well as the functions of agency deputy chiefs or other senior officials as COOs and members of the council. Leadership of the council now, as before, resides in the deputy director for management at OMB; the council's basic purposes, too, have not substantially changed since 1993: coordinate management policy across the executive branch, discuss common management problems, and exchange information (box 2-2). "We deal with management issues that cross, that impact the entire federal government, that are germane to all agencies," Johnson says.

» We focus on the President's Management Agenda. It's about establishing the desired management practices that the [agenda] calls for. The President's Management Council is a meeting every other month (an executive committee meets monthly), it's an e-mail list, it's a group of people that I, sitting at my computer, can talk to—about practices, something we ought to do, let me

> know what you think about this. We have established many ways of staying in touch with one another.

Three committees of the council oversee executive branch execution of the President's Management Agenda. One covers budget and performance integration and the improvement of financial performance. The second drives the expansion of electronic government, and the third addresses the strategic management of human capital and competitive sourcing. "To me, the management council is a part of the President's Management Agenda," Johnson says. "We're talking about how to better realize the dream, the opportunity associated with getting to green on all the PMA initiatives. It's almost exclusively focused on implementation of the management agenda."

Coordination

Today, federal management strategy operates essentially at two levels. First is the continuous dialogue between individual agencies and the OMB budget examiners, who play complicated roles of adviser, overseer, and enforcer in agency performance. This is the bedrock of the management process. Here each year, as they have for decades, the goals of an administration take shape and move forward. Programs fashioned by federal agencies to reflect administration policy are expressed in dollar and budget terms, undergo revision to accommodate congressional input during the budget process, and proceed to implementation, with constant OMB monitoring and fine-tuning. Former deputy secretary of transportation Michael Jackson provides a succinct, level-headed view of this process:

> » Dealing with OMB is a contact sport. You have to suit up and go play. It's a continual give-and-take, a constant battle, working through budget issues that each department needs to resolve in order to do its business. It's understandable and predictable and a normal part of doing business in a cabinet agency. You have to be prepared to be a very strong advocate and a creative advocate. And at the end of the day, after decisions are made, the president needs people to go out and support what the administration has agreed is best.

The other level of management strategy is the work of coordinating entities that have emerged over a number of years under the general leadership and oversight of the deputy director for management at OMB. With the President's Management Council leading the list, they range from older groups like the Joint Financial Management Improvement Program and the President's Council on Integrity and Efficiency to more recently prominent bodies such as councils, profiled in chapter 3, that bring together department and agency financial officers, information officers, and human capital officers. Meeting every few weeks, these and additional bodies are supposed to serve as coordinating channels for running the business of government, their work currently framed by the government-wide President's Management Agenda. They also offer forums for senior functional managers—career civil servants and political appointees alike—to trade ideas, learn from one another, and bond professionally.

OMB Deputy Director for Management Clay Johnson describes the tandem fashion in which these two levels—central coordination and OMB-agency dialogue—try to advance the administration's management and budget goals today.

» All the work with the agencies is done through the [OMB] branch examiners. . . . So, directly through the President's Management Council, we try to establish a big picture for the senior leadership of all the agencies. Then we try to equip the branches to be real smart at working through their counterparts at the lower levels in the agencies, to help the agencies get to the big long-term goals that we separately have been able to sell to their top management.

Each of the half dozen other coordinating groups under discussion here has its own director or leader, who organizes and runs its ongoing work. But as the chair or executive chair of all of them, including the PMC, Johnson is a good spokesman for the merits of the coordinating concept. "It makes perfect sense to get all the people together who are dealing with similar issues," Johnson reflects. "You're trying to get a clean audit, you're trying to close your books in forty-five days. Or you're trying to implement some part of the management agenda. The issues are the same."

Collectively he describes the several councils, including the PMC, as "mechanisms for sharing best and worst practices and being able to communicate quickly and effectively with everybody." To him, one of the advantages of coordinating the management work of many agencies is the chance to learn from everyone. "We make sure there's plenty of time to socialize and get to know one another. You shouldn't try to cure cancer in your agency by yourself. You should try to figure out if other agencies have already gotten through this roadblock, how they did it, and maybe learn from them, get through it better than they did."

Rather than groups with responsibilities or powers, Johnson views the councils he oversees as "communication facilitation mechanisms. We're in the marketing and facilitation-of-change business. We're there to help people learn faster than they might be able to otherwise" about why their agencies would run more efficiently and spend budget resources more effectively if they adopted a given approach. "We communicate why successful agencies have proven successful and why those that are lagging behind are lagging behind. Our idea is to make their learning curve very steep to facilitate the adoption of these policies."

Defining Success

Johnson believes that changing management in the current environment requires a clear definition of success and of the steps necessary to get there. Tough questions need realistic answers. Who is responsible for each step—not what group of people, but what one person? What process should hold that person accountable? In the case of homeland security, for example, when a truck approaches the U.S. border carrying something that might pose a threat, what should happen that doesn't happen now?

Once defined, success happens only with "total, unconditional commitment by the top" to achieving it. "The key for the credibility of the whole focus on management is that you have specific, outcome-related goals," Johnson says. Merely trying does not suffice. "You have a clean audit, or you don't. You're managing your information technology projects within 10 percent of the budget, or you're not. Eighty percent of your IT systems are secure, or they're not."

That underlines an obvious but important truth. Important as they are, the methods used to drive effective management—currently, the President's Management Agenda and coordination from the center—are less critical than what they produce. When he talks about taking unequivocal dead aim at results, Johnson is speaking not only for his administration. He is also articulating views forged in the years-long experience of thoughtful people in government and business alike, people at the core of a broad, nonpartisan consensus where the Government Performance and Results Act also found support. Having long ago rejected process as an end in itself, these expert thinkers and practitioners see desired outcomes as the goal that matters most. As an assistant secretary running an agency with a $46 billion annual budget put it, "Good intentions are better than bad intentions. But good intentions are not enough. You need to measure the results."

"When we first started focusing on results with agencies, they were very resistant," Johnson says. But they came to understand they would not be held responsible for programs that had not worked in the past. "We do expect them to help us figure out how to make them work, and be a part of the solution and not the problem. They learned that a focus on results was not to be feared."

The Impact

How do the people most involved—members of the President's Management Council, heads of the other coordinating councils, senior agency officials—view the processes driving federal management and their effects? How have people and agencies reacted to and been affected by the President's Management Agenda and the operations of the coordinating councils? How can the coordination process be improved?

Amid answers that vary widely, it's useful to put the President's Management Agenda and the coordinating mechanisms into some perspective. The PMA, with its program assessment rating tool and green-yellow-red management scorecard, constitutes the most aggressive executive attempt yet to boost the quality and return on investment of government programs—to get results that are order-of-magnitude better and more cost-effective. The PMA exerts its impact with direct, compulsory authority. Harnessed to and guided by that central mandate, the President's Management Council and its colleague coordinating groups seek to bring government's management functions into closer alignment and consistency, enabling better-informed managers to pursue the agenda more effectively. As vehicles for coordination, information, support, cooperation, collegiality, and promotion, the councils by their nature wield a less direct, controlling, or precise impact.

Like any structure, the overall process has strengths and weaknesses. As this is written, it rates a net favorable in the comments of practitioners around the federal establishment and observers with whom we talked. Here are some snapshots of what people are thinking and doing.

Not surprisingly, the mandatory nature of the President's Management Agenda and its scorecard has been an energizer. When he arrived at the Department of Health and Human Services (HHS), Assistant Secretary for Children and Families Wade Horn says his agency wasn't getting good marks on the scorecard. "And I became bound and determined that we were going to start getting good marks. We are now on our fifth consecutive quarter of all greens on all five items. I know we're the only operating division in HHS that has gotten this. And I'm very proud of it."

Budget Director Jolene Lauria-Sullens of the Department of Justice is the agency lead for the budget and performance integration initiative under the PMA (she also cochairs the cross-government Budget Officers Advisory Council, described in chapter 3). "A lot of financial data and performance information had not been connected heretofore," Lauria-Sullens says. The work of the integration initiative has "very much impacted" her work at Justice, "causing us to think about doing our budgets in a different way, think about selling the budget differently." In addition, "we are involved in virtually every PMA initiative. All the initiatives are discussed, worked on, and reported to OMB. They're either changing the way we do business or making us rethink the way we're doing business."

Inspector General Joseph Schmitz at the Defense Department thinks the President's Management Agenda carries the same weight as "an expressed statutory duty." His office has incorporated the agenda's five priorities into its strategic plan, together with the Defense Department's own priorities. In his quarterly reports to the secretary of defense, he categorizes his organization's results within these five priorities. That shows, Schmitz says, "not only what results we're achieving but how they are serving the bigger priorities of the administration."

While PMA initiatives need agency-by-agency implementation, said Deputy Secretary of Energy Kyle McSlarrow, success in doing that "to a very large degree required us to band together." The President's Management Council "has really allowed us to share experience across departments," where a less formal process might not have permitted it, he added. A member of the PMC's e-government committee, McSlarrow (as quoted in a chapter by Lily Kim in *The Business of Government,* published in 2003 by the IBM Center for the Business of Government) said the PMC is "really the engine driving management reforms."

But Michael Jackson, former deputy secretary of transportation, gives the PMC only "moderately effective marks" and draws a parallel between PMC meetings and those of the cabinet. "Cabinet meetings are typically occasions when the president essentially shares information. The President's Management Council was our equivalent of cabinet meetings in that they were in my view mostly informational. There were briefings about what somebody was doing on a specific management problem."

By contrast, he sees bodies like the National Security Council, the National Economic Council, and the Domestic Policy Council as "venues to deliberate about a specific issue, typically involving a subset of the entire cabinet." In his view, these were the meetings "where you really ground through the policy issues that were important to individual members." In the deputies' committees of those councils—the subsets—"you tend to have what I would call a more policy, budgetary, and substantive set of institutional tools to resolve those types of issues."

The President's Management Council, Jackson said, "was focused on one or two things routinely, like the President's Management Agenda initiatives. But it tended to be more sharing stories about people that did things and reporting news you could use." He adds that the principals of the PMC (the deputies) "did not as routinely show up at those meetings as they would maybe for some of those others. Probably on any given day half or a third sent a substitute." Jackson himself attended council meetings about 60 percent of the time. Was the President's Management Council useful to him as deputy secretary and chief operating officer at the Department of Transportation? "It was useful, but it didn't help you resolve the COO's daily problems that usually loomed high on your radar screen." Still, Jackson says, council meetings "were good by most people's accounts. It's maybe not the most viable of the tools that you have to do your business, but it's an important tool that helps organize the deputies—sort of a whip system for what we're going to do on these ten issues."

What improvements should be made? "Well, it's hard to accomplish the management work of the department in an (interagency) setting," Jackson says, "because the respective needs of each of the parties have a highly different focus. It's OMB's way of stimulating conversation about the particular set of agenda items that OMB has responsibility for in improving the management of government."

As for budget and performance integration, Jackson thinks that sometimes the types of measurements being used may not be sufficiently focused. "An example in my department was this great alignment between our safety goals in reducing highway fatalities and the budget to do that. But the measure of how many people died in the year was virtually meaningless to me as a tool of success. It was not a sufficiently focused measurement of what really needed to be done." He explains it this way: California's mandatory seat belt law has generated about a 91 percent usage rate, while some other states' usage rates register in the 50 percent range. "If everybody got to California's usage rate, we could have saved five or six thousand lives last year," Jackson says. "So if you asked what I wanted to know about aligning assets against performance, it was this: how are we going to persuade the rest of these states to pass a mandatory seat belt law?"

Given what he calls a "philosophic disinclination" to get mandatory legislation at the federal level, "we were going to offer carrots rather than sticks to get states there and also use the bully pulpit to try to talk that through. We needed more detailed metrics describing the legislative status in every state, what we could do in that state to help, and a time line for decisions by each legislature." That's what he means by a "focused measurement" of the task. It's one thing to complain about the situation, Jackson said, "but unless you go out and figure out the things that can actually change it and then measure them in a more granular way, you're not going to get anywhere."

For Samuel Bodman, deputy secretary of the Treasury and the department's chief operating officer, one of the PMC's biggest benefits has been "the personal relationships that have evolved. The deputies all know one another quite well." Before coming to Treasury, Bodman had the same responsibilities at the Department of Commerce and has served on the executive committee of the PMC from the beginning. He says the PMC has maintained "a fairly consistent approach. We have a quarterly dinner with our spouses and everyone has gotten to know one another." No one pretends that deputies and COOs in various agencies would not connect with one another if the PMC didn't exist. But the personal relationships it fosters, Bodman says, clearly facilitate the contacts necessary to do business. When an issue arose between his department and the Social Security Administration, "I just put in a call to Jim Lockhart, who's the deputy over at the Social Security Administration. Jim sits on the PMC executive committee. I see him regularly, and we're friends. That makes it easier to get things done. He called me back right away, and I explained to him what the problem was. We have a ready means of communicating."

Bodman sees the PMC as "a forum useful for describing best practices, describing progress, celebrating successes, criticizing failures," with the director of OMB appearing regularly to update members on budget and other issues and answer questions. It was the PMC, he recalls, that was "the vetting place for the [Program Assessment Rating Tool] program" as well as "the famous, or infamous, red, yellow, green buttons that indicate progress or lack thereof in various initiatives." The PMC is an arena "for learning, where people who have not had a lot of direct management can learn something about the problems that they face, some of the areas where they're good, and some of the areas where they're not so good, and where they stand to make improvement."

Some see the still-consolidating Department of Homeland Security—DHS—as a prototype of the coordinating function embodied in the new management strategy. One of them is the department's chief of staff,

Duncan Campbell. "As you look at the President's Management Agenda, the issues of setting up the twenty-first-century management structures and practices," he says, "we're in a position to really define it, to bring our twenty-two agencies together into one streamlined effort." He quotes Secretary of Homeland Security Thomas Ridge: "We're a divestiture, a start-up, a merger and acquisition, all at the same time," and says, "We've got all these disparate systems that we're trying to fuse into one. You've got entities that came from other departments, and entities that were created from scratch." As GAO chief David Walker puts it, the creation of the Department of Homeland Security is "the largest merger since creation of the Department of Defense and our current intelligence system in 1947."

A glance at the department's organization chart bears him out. It shows six main directorates: Information Analysis and Infrastructure Protection; Border and Transportation Security; Science and Technology; Management and Budget; Emergency Preparedness and Response; and Citizenship and Immigration Services. Into that sprawling structure, along with other entities, disappeared all of the twenty-two elements Campbell mentions, migrating from the Departments of Justice, Commerce, and Energy, among others. They included, for example, two large, well-known organizations—the Immigration and Naturalization Service and the Federal Emergency Management Agency. Thirteen other offices, tasked with such responsibilities as state and local outreach, the private sector, international affairs, legislative affairs, public affairs, and legal affairs, report directly to the secretary. Further complicating the task of managing DHS are the eighty-odd congressional committees and subcommittees with jurisdiction over components of the department.

Bringing all this together into one cohesive agency almost amounts to cross-government coordination by itself. It won't happen overnight or without titanic effort, says Campbell. "You rely on the leadership of the department to try to break down the cultures that existed pre-9/11 and pre-DHS. It really depends on the leadership exhibited by the senior members of the department. Each day it's getting better. But I'm not going to lie to you. It's a huge job."

It would be hard to underestimate its magnitude. David Walker of the GAO notes that the Department of Defense, created in 1947, brought together elements that were "all basically in the same lines of business." But only some of the twenty-plus agencies crowding under the Department of Homeland Security's roof are "full time in the homeland security line of business. Others are very much part time in that line of business. Trying to merge all those different types of cultures and systems is a major challenge."

When he became acting deputy secretary of education (he was later appointed and confirmed as deputy secretary), Eugene Hickok found the President's Management Council generally useful. "I wasn't engaged in these conversations much until I became acting deputy," he says. "It's useful as sort of a benchmark, to get a sense of what other agencies are doing, how they take on their challenges." When we talked with him, however, Hickok believed the No Child Left Behind program (a key domestic priority of the George W. Bush administration) deserved most of his time and energy. "I've got to take my priorities where they are and the president's priority is implementation of this law. In the long run, in my opinion, the American people will judge us more on the implementation of No Child Left Behind."

While he put the PMC high on his list, he said "the responsibilities of running this organization" drove his agenda. "People in management responsibilities," he noted, "should be there doing their jobs, because that's what their jobs are, not because a management council is out there telling them what to worry about." That's not to say the council is not important, Hickok stated. "We need to be more business-like. We need to look at the bottom line. We need to look at performance. We need to look at the civil service system, the personnel system, the contracting system, the resource management system."

At the Defense Department, Inspector General Schmitz drew on the model of another coordinating council—the President's Council on Integrity and Efficiency (PCIE), of which he is a member—to set up a mini-version within the military establishment. It's a special story worth telling.

The PCIE groups agency inspectors general appointed by the president, including Schmitz. It is, in his words, "a trade association for federal inspectors general." As he explains it, the mini-PCIE within his department developed from language in the 1978 legislation that created inspectors general. A separate section of that act makes clear that the Defense IG has the responsibility to collaborate with the inspectors general of the individual military departments and their audit, inspection, and investigatory elements.

"None of those component heads worked for me," Schmitz recalls, "but under the Inspector General Act [of 1978], I had an affirmative duty to cooperate with them. There was really nothing structural in place to do that." So he decided to brief them soon after each regular PCIE meeting "to share what I had just gotten at the White House." This gathering soon grew into the Defense Council on Integrity and Efficiency—DCIE—a microcosm of the PCIE within the Department of Defense. "We literally took the charter for the PCIE and cut and pasted," Schmitz says. Then came the realization there were other people, not specifically identified in the Inspector General Act, who were not included but should be. These were the inspectors general of the Defense Department's four intelligence agencies and representatives of the Joint Chiefs of Staff and the National Guard Bureau. "Because of the nature of what they do, they fit in the same category as people in the same business throughout the department," he says. "They all wanted to come." Result: members of the DCIE number about sixteen.

"It's been very well received," Schmitz thinks; "principals actually showing up for these meetings. We actually circulated the PCIE charter to make sure it wasn't just an edict from me, that everybody actually agreed to it, and formally approved it." After he passes along the main points of the previous PCIE meeting, a general discussion gives DCIE members a chance to talk about anything they're doing related to the issues the PCIE is focusing on. They can showcase their own work, including best practices, and learn what their colleagues are doing. "It has been a good tool for helping them do their jobs," Schmitz adds.

» It forces us, on a monthly basis, to get face time. You can talk all you want about staffs cooperating, but when the component heads never meet, it's hard to say you're really cooperating. We try to raise issues early, before the train wrecks. We try to do it the way the PCIE does. As I said, none of these people work for me, and I really don't have direct authority to order them to come over here. So we've done this as a reach-out among equals, to do something that benefits all of us.

But the impact of the DCIE doesn't end there. Well beyond its information sharing and coordination services, it has become instrumental in the training and greater professionalism of the inspector general function within the U.S. military establishment. Across the Defense Department, some 1,250 civilian and military officials work in inspector general operations. Much of their training is redundant; in fact, the Army, Navy, and Air Force each run an inspector general academy. The situation begged for elimination of overlaps and sharing of best practices. In Schmitz's own operation, meanwhile, about thirty professionals were benefiting from a part-time, three-year master's degree program run by visiting faculty of Central Michigan University. He looked into the possibility of shaping a better-tailored program, "a master's in public administration focused on

IGs in the broader sense" that would be open to people from component offices as well as his own.

After conversations with local universities as well as a competition among them, Georgetown University emerged as the site of a new, two-year program. "Our people are actually going to get Georgetown master's degrees out of this," Schmitz says. "The course is functionally designed to help us be better auditors, inspectors, and investigators. We've proved the paradigm within our own staff, and next time we opened up ten of the thirty slots to the component elements." The new program attracted twice as many applicants as it could handle. "We literally had to set up a graduate admissions program and meet the Georgetown standards," Schmitz says. He challenged the students to write their theses on issues that could be published in the *Journal of Inquiry,* the PCIE trade journal. The Georgetown program is one example of what he believes will be the maturing of the DCIE into "more than just meeting on a monthly basis."

Speaking of the CFO Council and his colleagues working in government financial management, Department of State chief financial officer Christopher Burnham sees

> » a large piece that we all have in common. Getting us together to share best practices, to receive guidance directly from OMB on where the president wants us to go, particularly concerning the President's Management Agenda, is essential. I found [the CFO Council] very valuable as a place to come in and share ideas. Without that, you personally wouldn't know your counterparts in other agencies. It's so much easier to call up a counterpart and say, what are you doing down there at your agency, I know you won an award or you got an accolade, and can we come over and learn a little bit about that? There are number of ways we're seeing that, such as those who are getting to green on improved financial performance.

"They have done educational activities, outreach, surveys, and feedback, and held some seminars in conjunction with Council for Excellence in Government, which have been very helpful," Burnham says. "I think we assume that we come to these jobs and know everything there is to know, which is hardly the case."

The CFO Council could strengthen its impact, he feels, with a greater focus on education. "We should have a dose of ethics training every year. I think that Sarbanes-Oxley–like rules will eventually be applied to all of us," he adds, referring to legislation in 2002 that brought significant changes to corporate financial practice and corporate governance regulation. "Of course, that's never completely applicable to government, because we don't have a profit motive. But I do believe that we now need to run with the same kind of leadership in the public sector that Sarbanes-Oxley has imposed on the private sector."

Karen Alderman directs the Joint Financial Management Improvement Program—JFMIP—created by statute in the late 1940s. She sees her organization, originally focused on improving accounting practices, as "a precedent that established the concept of collaborative action for making cross-government improvements." Many current cross-cutting initiatives, she says, lack the institutional framework that would allow them to survive from administration to administration. "That is one of the benefits this organization has: a long history and a legislative and statutory framework. . . . . Cross-cutting institutions in government require some kind of institutional legitimacy to operate over the long haul. You need a statutory and institutional basis. And you don't get it just like that. You have to build it. It helps to have a framework that allows you to withstand the pressures that always come with a change of administration."

Before the 1990 legislation that established the Chief Financial Officers Council, the JFMIP was the only significant, ongoing link between agencies that shared common financial management issues and requirements. With the CFO Council in operation, Alderman has worked regularly with it and its subordinate committees "to help move things along." In 1996, Alderman says, the Federal Financial Management Improvement Act institutionalized requirements developed by the JFMIP "as a foundation that agencies must comply with."

As with other administrative functions of government, she says the government financial management community's expectations of higher quality, as well as its changing components and business processes, reflect rapidly changing technology and the challenges of integration. These needs are finding responses at the JFMIP and the CFO Council. In the financial management environment, which cross-cuts all of government, they have changed a great deal since 1990, in statute and through accounting standards, Alderman says. The same phenomena that affect all systems, like the Internet and information security issues, are affecting financial management systems. "Financial reporting requirements are increasing," Alderman says; "standards are getting tougher. The first financial statements were produced six months after the close of the fiscal year. In 2004, the government-wide financial statement must be produced within forty-five days."

What has made that particular change happen is not more people to do the work; in fact, there are fewer people. "The processes, the systems, and the planning are better," Alderman says; "and this all on the financial reporting side. There's another whole issue": do program managers get the financial information in time to support decisionmaking on programs, budget execution, cost accounting, cost management, and control? "These are tough problems that cross all these different agencies. It's been a continuous challenge, and part of the work we do has helped communicate the building blocks, in a standard way."

John Higgins, inspector general of the Department of Education, advises his agency's executive management team, among whose members are the deputy secretary, the under secretary, and a few assistant secretaries. "They are basically implementing the President's Management Agenda," he says. "I give them advice, I try to tell them where we [the inspector general's office] don't think they're complying with the management agenda, give them our suggestions on how they can improve compliance." Higgins also serves on the auditing committee of the President's Council on Integrity and Efficiency. "A lot of the issues there are definitely governmentwide," he says. "We have a lot of auditing requirements that every IG has to comply with in every agency. So it's very useful to discuss how the different agencies are doing things."

The example he cites concerns the ways in which various IGs are approaching the audits required under the Federal Information Systems Management Act. "Half are conducting them as evaluations, and half are doing audit testing," Higgins notes. "We're going to take this up with the audit committee and try to standardize it, so we are all doing it the same way in the different agencies. From the perspective of the Chief Financial Officers Council, I think they would like to see some consistency."

Higgins says he benefits from hearing "the different issues that are before the members of the PCIE, hearing what the other IGs have to say. Sometimes we don't have the luxury of reinventing the wheel all the time, and we can hear how other IGs are doing things. It saves us time and money to hear what they're doing, pick up their ideas." Sometimes his positions on issues change "because I get information I didn't have before, or I've heard things from other IGs that I was not aware of. It's just plain interesting to hear other perspectives on some of the issues. The Council is getting more efficient. Every time we meet, it gets better."

For Clark Kent Ervin, inspector general of the Department of Homeland Security, one of the most helpful efforts of the PCIE has been the work to draft amendments to the Inspector General Act, "to come up with a model IG act for improvements." For example, "there has been helpful discussion about peer reviews," in which one inspector general inspects another IG's audit or investigative shop on a prescribed and published schedule. In the same vein, the PCIE has explored such a peer review process for inspections as well. "Peer reviews for everything an inspector general does are very healthy," Ervin comments.

Ervin says recent presentations at PCIE meetings have been particularly good and especially relevant to the inspector general community, "as opposed to just a topic of general government." Agreeing with Higgins's favorable assessment of the council, Ervin says the PCIE provides an invaluable opportunity to get together, to get to know each other, and to "pick each other's brains" about issues of common interest.

Having a centralized way to discuss and describe management challenges and progress is essential, says Clinton administration veteran Edward DeSeve, and "the idea of a management agenda is therefore a very important idea." Reflecting on the antecedents to current management methodology that emerged in the 1990s, he notes the concepts and goals embodied in programs like the Clinton-era National Performance Review and in what were called "major management challenges." In response to those, "agencies on an agency-specific basis, or on a systemic basis, agreed as part of the annual budget submission to go forward and do things. We tried to develop those cooperatively with the bodies involved." Thus if information security was a high-level issue, "we worked to develop a solution for information security that a large group of people bought into, felt ownership of. So it was more a cooperative venture in solving problems that were both cross-cutting and agency-specific."

"What I've heard from agencies," DeSeve adds, "is that the President's Management Agenda has functioned more as a series of edicts—for example, in areas such as competitive sourcing—rather than a cooperatively agreed upon plan for agencies and the central administration to follow." That is not true across the board, he says, "but where there's been a weakness in the approach, it's that it's a directive rather than a cooperative management engagement." Not that there shouldn't be a central document or central vision, he says; every president is entitled to have one. In his administration, for instance, "we got [the Government Performance and Results Act] passed, we got all the e-government apparatus put in place, the revisions to the OMB A76 regulations, the precursors to competitive sourcing. The only thing we probably didn't spend as much time on is human capital. Anyway, they're following through on things we began, which we think is a great thing."

Managing: Final Comments

» There's a temptation in government jobs to think of success as "I got money in my in box and I put money into my out box." Managers asked to describe their programs are apt to say they get X amount of money and are very pleased to report that they were able to get it out the door in Y number of months. Asked what was accomplished, the reply is "Well, that's not really my job. I just get the money out the door. Congress gave it to us, told us how to spend it, and we did." But just getting money out is a process-oriented perspective on being a good manager, which affects too many people in government jobs, political or nonpolitical.

People also say we can't do something better because of an existing law. To which my customary answer was, that may be the damn law, but let's tell somebody about it and see if we can get it changed. And sometimes we can. In a surprising number of cases, you can if you just really work it, and make a decent case. If someone says it needs an executive order, that's not an excuse for inaction—let's just go make the case and work it, and two or three months later we may have our executive order. My advice to colleagues who decide to go into government jobs is not to consider the status quo an immovable object. If things need to be moved, then bash into them with gusto. [Michael Jackson, deputy secretary of transportation, George W. Bush administration, 2001–03]

» There is no way, when you start to talk about organizations of the size of federal agencies, that you can really manage them from a single point. All you can do is provide leadership, guidance, and coordination. The work has to be done by the people who are, in fact, living with the systems and with the problems. And those are the people in the agencies. [John Koskinen, deputy director for management, Office of Management and Budget, Clinton administration]

CHAPTER 3

Coordinating Groups

Just as the President's Management Council, beginning in the Clinton administration, has played the senior, overarching coordination role, most of the other councils take similar approaches for senior managers across government in the functional areas of finance, budget, information technology, human resources, efficiency and integrity, and acquisition. Anyone examining what these groups are supposed to do will be struck by the extent to which they (and agency positions with corresponding responsibilities) are links in each other's chains. Their issues, decisions, and work often have common concerns and are in some specific cases intertwined. This is especially true in the area of workforce management, an issue of prime relevance to government's performance and one that engages senior functional managers and management coordinators everywhere. It's not surprising, therefore, that these interagency groups regularly share information, experience, and views, sometimes in joint meetings. They cross-fertilize in other ways as well—the Chief Acquisition Officers Council, for instance, has subcommittees on e-government, financial management, human capital, and competitive sourcing. All such practices tend to strengthen the impact of the councils.

The Chief Financial Officers Council

In the 1980s chief financial officers could be found in a number of federal agencies that had hired them to fill perceived needs in budget planning and finance. These individuals in 1987 set up an advisory group—a roundtable to think about common issues like modernizing financial systems and improving the quality of financial information. In establishing the Chief Financial Officers Council three years later, the CFO Act formalized that effort. The essential purpose was collaboration to improve U.S. federal financial management.

Under the legislation, the new council was instructed to reach consensus, as a "senior-level forum," on the policies and priorities of good financial management and to communicate these findings to other senior officials within the executive branch. It was to advise and coordinate agencies staffed with chief financial officers in working toward consolidation and modernization of financial systems; better quality of financial information, financial data, and information standards; instituting internal controls; and drafting legislation affecting financial operations and organizations. The council's chair is the controller in OMB's Office of Federal Financial Management (under the executive chairmanship of OMB's deputy director for management). Council members are the CFOs and deputy CFOs of twenty-five cabinet departments and agencies, as well as senior OMB and Treasury Department officials. Representatives of the Government Accountability Office and the President's Council on Integrity and Efficiency (discussed below) sit in as ex officio members; representatives of the Joint Financial Management Improvement Program, the Small Agency Council, and the Private Sector Council (a nongovernmental group) attend as observers. Five council committees address issues in the areas of financial management policies and practices, best practices, erroneous payments, acceleration of financial statements, performance measurement, and e-government.

Early in its life the CFO Council evolved from a group led by OMB into a body primarily directed by its members, according to Edward DeSeve, deputy director for management at OMB from 1998 to 2001. The council, he says, moved "from being a site receiving a broadcast to a network of mutually reinforcing individuals with their own agenda."

Some idea of how that happened emerged in an article by Mike Serlin in the May 1996 issue of *Government Executive* magazine. A government official at the time, Serlin described an initiative begun by several CFOs and deputy CFOs, both career and political, that "jump-started the process." With OMB officials and other members of the federal financial management community, the group examined opportunities "to transform the passive CFO Council into a vehicle for more active cooperation among agencies dealing with common problems." Then, over lunch with the CFOs and deputy CFOs of several departments in early 1994, the group presented "a strategy to transform and re-energize the CFO Council." Its recommendations included setting the agenda for monthly meetings in coordination with OMB staff, "rather than simply being informed of the agenda," and broadening council membership "to include both CFOs, who were mostly political appointees, and career deputy CFOs to ensure cooperation and continuity of effort beyond the average two-year tenure of political appointees." Serlin noted that the full council adopted the plan with the complete support of the council's chair.

During the years that followed, according to one agency CFO we interviewed, "the council's agenda was set by working with the agencies. I thought it was a very effective tool at that time for problem solving and creating a community of CFOs." The group was not seen as, and was not, a vehicle for OMB to "press its will on the CFOs," this official says. Then, in this view, the council's status reverted to what it had been originally. Today's council "is not run in a particularly collegial fashion. And maybe that's the proper role for it. But I've not found it, in my experience, to be an effective problem-solving tool."

How can the situation be improved? The official agrees that one proper role for the council is to serve as "an instrument of OMB to communicate policies," and adds: "That's only one role. I think it can also be a problem-solving forum across agencies, which means that OMB has to cede some power in that regard. I think it can also be an idea-gathering body. And that, I think, is probably one of its most important functions. It's a cultural idea—how do we want to use this? Do we want to use it as an information exchange, one-way, two-way? Or do we want to use it as a problem-solving body? Do we want to use it as an idea-gathering body? Or do we want to try all three?"

Along the way, the CFO Council did design a set of goals and strategies that offers a more precise idea of what it is trying to do. For example, to strengthen the government-wide framework that provides sound financial policy and services, the council is to oversee the functions and coordination among central agencies as well as between central agencies and program agencies. To continually raise the use of modern technology and business practices within the financial management community, the strategy calls on the council to "benchmark with ourselves and other high-performance organizations." To produce high-quality financial information in support of financial and performance reporting, the council should create a system "for integrating performance measures, cost information, and financial reporting." It should also establish "integrated government financial management systems which minimize data entry and human intervention."

The Budget Officers Advisory Council

Members of the Budget Officers Advisory Council (the BOAC), which came into being in 1996, are the senior career budget officials in OMB and in the cabinet departments and major independent agencies. The council acts as a forum to informally exchange ideas and discuss issues of interest. Topics range from technical and conceptual matters to the operational concerns of budget accounting, formulation, and execution. The BOAC normally convenes monthly.

"We talk about policies that impact current budget operations and future planned budgets," says Jolene Lauria-Sullens, budget director at the Justice Department and BOAC chair. "Sometimes we have people talk about the financial audit closeout or the performance and accountability reports. It's really pretty much an open agenda, and can vary in topical area, because in the budget field, almost everything touches budget—if you don't have funding, you can't operate your program. There's very little that doesn't have a hook to a budget officer position. Having the ability via the BOAC to query the folks that are setting the policy for government and facilitating it, I think that's the major benefit."

She adds that the information shared in these meetings is "more down to our organizations than up." But members can bring up and present issues to OMB. A recent agenda, for example, included a topic on "how to do funds control in the new age." She explains that "everybody in government is limited and is controlled by the apportionment process, which constricts how much funding you can spend." But the current OMB process is paper-intensive. Transmitting hard-copy signed authority to agencies to spend money that Congress has appropriated depends on fax machines. "It might take a long time for a program manager in the field to get authority to spend money on a given day that Congress appropriates on a given day," Lauria-Sullens says. "You're supposed to have ten days for the documents to be signed, but it very rarely takes only ten days, particularly when you trace the process end to end, from appropriation to program spending. In these times, that's certainly not how to get documents signed and cleared."

When we talked with her, that problem was on the BOAC agenda. "We're thinking about coming up with a streamlined and changed process. The specific way that the document creates funding controls or limitations is being discussed—should it be more flexible, given that auditing and accounting has more constraints on it, more reporting now than it ever had? Maybe we will reconsider the whole document, which would be a big deal for the entire government."

On the content of BOAC meetings, she says "information sharing is two ways. Information sharing shouldn't just be from the talking heads that run the council, it should be both ways. I think if we want to improve, it would be better if there were more two-way conversations, where there is more active participation. A lot of people come to listen and take notes. If I were to change that, members would contribute more than just listening." Not everyone is comfortable putting their positions on the table, she recognizes. But "if we were to improve, that would be the area."

The Chief Information Officers Council

Established in 1996 by executive order and formalized by statute under the E-Government Act of 2002, the Chief Information Officers Council (the CIO Council) seeks to help agencies do a better job in the design, acquisition, development, modernization, use, and sharing of government's information technology resources. The council's responsibilities trace not only to the E-Government Act but also to objectives defined in the Government Performance and Results Act (1993); the Information Technology Management Reform Act (1996), more widely known as the Clinger-Cohen Act; and the Paperwork Elimination Act (1999).

As associate director of OMB for e-government and information technology 2001–03, Mark Forman also headed the CIO Council. (With the 2002 establishment of OMB's Office of E-Government and IT, he became that office's first administrator.) At the beginning of his tenure in 2001, he says, the council "existed for communications and not for getting work done. One of the changes I put in place was making it a working body, with the work being the process of IT governance. That's unique among the cross-agency councils. I don't know of any other council that really sees itself as part of the management of the government." He doesn't downplay the value of consensus building or sharing best practices—processes that the council facilitates. But he points out that "consensus building, where it communicates the impact of a directive, isn't really getting work done. Consensus building where you move the objective forward—in other words, where you help achieve the objective—is what we did in the CIO Council."

Composed of major cabinet department and agency CIOs and deputy CIOs, the council has multiple tasks. It presents OMB with recommendations on information technology management policy and requirements. It assists OMB in shaping creative multiagency information technology projects that improve government performance, then helps coordinate their rollout. It leads efforts to broaden electronic government in the federal establishment. With OMB and the National Institute of Standards and Technology, the council seeks to maximize the use of commercial information technology standards, setting guidelines on such issues as interconnectivity, interoperability, and the efficiency and security of government computer systems. It develops and promotes the use of common performance measures in the management of agencies' information technology resources.

With the Office of Personnel Management, the CIO Council focuses on federal employees working in information technology—their hiring, classification, training, and professional development requirements. With the archivist of the United States, it explores the effective application of federal information technology resources to fulfill requirements of the Federal Records Act. The council supports the government's use of strategies developed in the private sector, such as continuous process improvement (constant adjustment of a process to improve it) and measurable increases in employee productivity. Karen Evans, a federal civil service veteran and former CIO of the Department of Energy who in 2003 succeeded Forman as administrator of OMB's Office of E-Government and Information Technology and director of the CIO Council, says the council "is very transparent in its operations, . . . with public minutes of its meetings, annual strategic plans, and numerous reports posted on its website at www.cio.gov." CIOs, she adds, "can talk with one another in real time" through the council's listserv.

"What I work to do is encourage CIOs to work together to accomplish these shared goals," Evans says. As a former chief information officer and vice chair of the CIO Council and now its leader, she believes that she has the perspective to judge its effectiveness. The council can count accomplishments on several fronts, in her view: "the strong and stable relationship that the council supports between OMB and agencies, the success of the twenty-four e-government projects [identified by OMB in 2001 and prioritized as the most promising government-wide initiatives], the common coordination in development of the Federal Enterprise Architecture [see chapter 5], and closer coordination of cybersecurity response." She sees the group as an important forum for chief information officers to resolve common problems and "communicate with OMB on policy and direction of federal information technology." For instance, "going into the development of fiscal year 2006 budget guidance, OMB had proposed a series of changes." But after gathering the views of the CIO community, she says, the council decided together to hold off on any proposed changes until fiscal year 2007 so that extensive changes begun under the fiscal year 2005 guidance could be completed.

John Koskinen, a deputy director for management at OMB in the Clinton administration, credits the CIO Council with providing the government-wide, coordinated effort that dealt efficiently with the Y2K challenge of the late 1990s—preparing for the anticipated computer programming crisis as the calendar crossed from the twentieth century into the twenty-first. Further, since 2001, the CIO Council has participated in OMB's first wave of e-government expansion under the President's Management Agenda (see the discussion of chief information officers in chapter 4).

In 2003, the CIO Council worked with OMB on publishing a set of enterprise architecture reference models (see chapter 5), used to spot opportunities for collaboration that permit more effective spending on information technology. It was also instrumental in OMB's incorporation of comments by federal chief information officers regarding authentication guidance for federal agencies in certain electronic transactions. Looking ahead, Evans sees key challenges for the CIO Council, and government generally, in "expanding the use of e-government practices, gaining more productivity for each IT investment, and strengthening cybersecurity."

How do the activities of the CIO Council relate to what's actually happening in agency programs? We asked Wade Horn, assistant secretary for children and families in the Administration on Children, Youth, and Families at the Department of Health and Human Services. Horn says that he "volunteered and pushed" his agency into the forefront of e-government:

» I think there are almost nothing but advantages to e-government. The only disadvantage is that you have to change, and change is not easy in any organizational structure. As promising as the alternative may be, what you're already doing is always more comfortable than where you're headed. On the other hand, it's just common sense to say the use of technology is the only thing that allows us to be able to do more with less. The reason why productivity goes up in the private sector is not because people are working longer hours, but because they're working more efficiently and effectively and smarter. And what allows them to do that is technology.

When we spoke with him, Horn used as an example of his agency's management of a number of grants in the Healthy Marriage Initiative program, including seven grants through child welfare, seven waivers of certain conditions in child support enforcement, and three demonstration projects in child support enforcement. In addition, the agency was about to announce the availability of funds for marriage education services and federal post-adoption services. "We also have marriage education grants through some of the refugee resettlement programs. So there are a lot of programs all looking at integrating marriage education into existing service-delivery programs." In the old days, he says, "you'd have each of those programs developing their own way of monitoring and providing technical assistance to these grants. And I'd have to go to each of these various offices and ask them for an update to be sure that we're doing a good job in providing technical assistance and oversight to these grants."

"Now we're in the process of developing a single web portal, which allows some flexibility, given that there are different goals of each of these various programs, but there's a common thread in terms of marriage education services." When the portal is completed, Horn says, employees in any agency office, or technical assistance providers, will be able to go to the web portal and, using a standardized format,

» input what they've done, and what the remaining issues might be, or what follow-up steps they're going to take. So, on a monthly basis, I'll get a report with the landscape of all the marriage education grantees and the frequency of contact with them. And right away, I'll be able to ask if we're ignoring any of them, or where the problems are, or if there are any constant themes across the various marriage education grantees. And it'll all be generated for me.

For the CIO Council and everyone else in the federal information technology community—both agency CIOs and the OMB's e-government office—Mark Forman offers important advice. He points to the movement toward web-based or shared services, a developing mechanism that he says will become the primary vehicle for collaboration across organizational boundaries. "Rarely will an agency have any application, any computer system need, that is so unique . . . that it will build a huge end-to-end system in itself." Instead, the system will generally be

» a combination of things the agency will build for itself with reuse of an application or a code that's being used by three or four or fifteen other agencies, just because the missions of government are redundant. The redundancy of missions has a major symptom—redundancy in IT investments and business processes. The web services architecture—people are calling it services-oriented architecture—is a fundamentally different way to integrate and collaborate across organizations and it's rippling through the economy.

Those coming into the government information technology community, he says, "have to be cognizant that this is the emerging architecture that they, too, should use."

In this, Forman is recognizing a fact of life—services-oriented architecture—that was also apparent to Clinton administration managers. One of them is Edward DeSeve, deputy director for management at OMB from 1998 to 2001. "When we set up, through legislation, the CIO Council and the CFO Council and the [President's Management Council], they were all in their day very innovative," he says. "They really looked at a new idea called network management, where we worked together with the individuals in the departments, giving them some of the authority of the president and OMB to get things done. The centrality of information and the use of real-time information to do things is enormously important," DeSeve maintains, and its importance will only grow over time. "It used to be that hierarchical dissemination from the leader out to the followers was an appropriate way to think about organizing something. Now we simply put information on nodes and on websites and ask people to use it. Once they start doing that, then the whole idea of shared services and being able to have individuals take responsibility for their own activities through the Internet is just there."

The Joint Financial Management Improvement Program

Collaborative steps to boost the quality of federal financial management practices began in the years just after World War II; it engaged the Bureau of the Budget (now OMB), the Department of the Treasury, and the General Accounting Office (now the Government Accountability Office), Congress's chief investigative and audit agency. The Budget and Accounting Procedures Act of 1950 gave this coalition statutory standing by establishing the Joint Financial Management Improvement Program (JFMIP). The Office of Personnel Management and the General Services Administration joined later. Representatives of the five agencies—"the principal management oversight arms of government," in the words of JFMIP Executive Director Karen Alderman—serve as a steering committee. They supply leadership and guidance for JFMIP activities, which are carried out by a ten-person staff. The committee also includes the executive director and a program agency delegate, who serves a two-year term. JFMIP's $3 million annual budget comes from the sponsoring agencies as well as—since 1999—from agencies covered by the Chief Financial Officers Act.

For the federal financial community, the JFMIP plays the role of catalyst, coordinator, clearinghouse, and critic. According to its official description, the program guides financial management improvement across government, promoting strategies, reviewing and coordinating the activities and policy promulgations of its sponsoring agencies, and disseminating information about good financial management practices. It convenes conferences and other instructional events, publishes a newsletter, and operates FinanceNet, an online electronic clearinghouse.

"We publish the functional requirements for all the financial systems in government," Alderman says. That includes core financial and personnel and payroll, as well as loans and direct loans—any money "that comes into the government, moves around the government, or goes out of the government. We issue those documents on behalf of the federal government. We have long-term business." The JFMIP also works on human capital issues relevant to its field, organizing processes and studies to identify workforce competencies for financial management.

In 1998, the JFMIP got statutory authority to set up a program management office that more than doubled its full-time staff. Partly reflecting its mandate to test and qualify commercial software products, this office develops systems requirements, gives agencies and vendors information necessary to improve financial systems, makes certain that products meet system requirements, and simplifies procurement. "The testing and qualifying of core financial system vendor software to ensure that it meets federal functionality is there in OMB policy," Alderman says. "It has a large impact in industry that can serve government. And there's a lot of money that rides on it, in terms of being able to sell to the government."

Alderman cites one JFMIP success story: core financial systems are among the most complex in the federal government. Five years ago, only two in ten such systems in development were being planned without customization—special code to meet individual agency needs. As Alderman points out, however, customization "drives up life-cycle costs and risk in any kind of system." In 2003, only two out of ten systems in development were being planned *with* customization, and "that's the impact of better requirements, better testing," she says. "The impact in terms of reducing the cost and risk of all federal agencies has been tremendous."

Another example of JFMIP's government-wide functionality is the updating of property system requirements, in which the Department of Defense has the lead. "We have people from all the major property-holding organizations in government participating," Alderman says, "systems people and program people." Once issued, the document becomes the new standard for property management with which federal financial systems must comply. "I've got one person who's managing the update process," she says. "The others are from all over the government."

What other cross-government issues in financial management present challenges? "One that I think is very significant is the workforce," Alderman replies. A recent JFMIP study looked at the future of the federal financial management workforce and what would be needed for the community to meet government's anticipated competency needs. Alderman thinks the study's analysis was correct but sees "no leadership in the community" to act on its recommendations. "There is no CFO Council Human Capital Subcommittee any more, and there's just very spotty focus on this workforce problem."

Offering some perspective on this concern, she says federal financial management does not lend itself to simple outsourcing. "You really have to have people that understand the legislative and management framework of financial management in the federal government, the fiscal accountability associated with both budget execution and cost management," she says. There are "brilliant people" in the private sector, but

> » if they don't have background in the types of accountability that come with the money appropriated by Congress, they don't know how to configure the systems. They don't know what the systems are supposed to do. They don't know what people will be held accountable for. They don't know how it flows through the entire enterprise. That's what financial management is. A lot of what the federal government does is bring money in, move money around to do something like deliver health care, or sends money out in loans, benefits, and grants. But it all comes with this accountability portion. You have to be able to capture the information and account for all that money.

The private sector does not have this type of accountability for the flow of resources, she says. "You need to have people educated, brought up, broadened. . . . And with 45 percent of your workforce over 50, unless you start doing something about that now, where are you going to get those people?" She sees the present workforce as dominated by "transaction processing in administrative areas." But systems will be doing those jobs in the future. "People are not going to be entering data and reconciling one system to another in the future. They should be analyzing what all that information means. People with those kinds of skills are what you need in the future. But where are they, and how are we going to get them? The failure to focus on that, I think, is a very big issue."

The President's Council on Integrity and Efficiency

A 1988 presidential executive order established the President's Council on Integrity and Efficiency for agency inspectors general appointed by the president. Four year later, another presidential order created the Executive Council on Integrity and Efficiency, whose membership comprises inspectors general appointed by agency heads. By their charters, the two groups range government-wide, looking for areas of vulnerability to fraud, waste, and abuse and designing programs to address those weaknesses and promote integrity and efficiency in government programs. The two councils also work to make a well-trained, skilled, professional inspector general workforce a reality. To those ends, members of both groups conduct interagency and intra-agency audit, inspection, and investigation projects and set policies and standards for problems that exceed the capability or jurisdiction of an individual agency.

A website sponsored by the two councils (www.ignet.gov) supplies inspectors general throughout the government with a variety of reports, support materials, and information. For example, the site's "What's New" page in June 2004 contained the following:

—A *Guide for Conducting Qualitative Assessment Reviews for Investigative Operations of Inspectors General*

—The newsletter of the Inspection and Evaluation Committee

—An update to an appendix of the *Guide for Conducting External Quality Control Reviews of the Audit Operations of Offices of Inspector General*

—Minutes and presentations from a roundtable on the Government Performance and Results Act

—A call for comments on the *Exposure Draft to Incorporate the Provisions of Statement on Auditing Standards 99, Consideration of Fraud in a Financial Statement Audit*

—A *Survey of Inspection and Evaluation Units in the Federal Inspector General Community*

—The annual report of the Inspection and Evaluation Committee

The deputy director for management at OMB chairs both the PCIE and the ECIE and appoints vice-chairs from their memberships to manage the councils' work. Also represented in both groups are the Federal Bureau of Investigation, the Office of Government Ethics, the Office of Special Counsel, and the Office of Personnel Management.

The Chief Human Capital Officers Council

Human capital? Human resources? The terms exemplify government's occasional tendency to turn meaning into gibberish or, in this case, people into things. We're talking here, of course, about the workforce, employees, human beings. They represent what is frequently and correctly called government's most important strength.

"More has happened in the human capital, or people strategy, area in the last two years than the last twenty-five years," says U.S. Comptroller General David Walker. To see why, begin by noting that management of the vast federal workforce ceased some time ago to be a set of rules and procedures that could be applied inflexibly across the public sector. Government's responsibilities today are simply too differentiated, complicated, interlocked, and global to accommodate a uniform set of standards and regulations. That's why federal agencies have been seeking—and have gained—considerable flexibility in personnel matters. Most recently, Congress, in establishing the Department of Homeland Security, exempted it from civil service rules on hiring, pay, promotion, and more. Congress also endorsed Department of Defense plans to redesign its civilian compensation system. There is widespread recognition that information technology levies its own special set of demands for employees who can use it effectively and exploit its potential.

The homeland security legislation of 2002 also established the Chief Human Capital Officers Council (the CHCO Council) and created chief human capital positions in major agencies. The legislation instructed the new body to coordinate the human capital functions of agencies and meet regularly with representatives of government employee unions. It directed the Office of Personnel Management (OPM) to design systems, including measurements, to evaluate agencies' management of their personnel. Chaired by the director of OPM, the CHCO Council is meant to be a high-level policy-planning body that seeks to advance the modernization of human resources systems, improve the quality of human resources information, and promote legislation affecting human resources operations and organizations. The director of OPM chairs the council with the oversight of the deputy director for management at OMB.

To that end, for example, the Department of State has been working with the CHCO Council and the OPM to accomplish some needed reforms. Robert Pearson, a veteran career diplomat who is director general of the foreign service and head of human resources at the State Department, notes that the "broad new goals" set by the council and the President's Management Agenda have provided leverage with his department's workforce to execute changes within the department's personnel management to get reform done. He also perceives helpful suppleness on the part of OPM. "Looking at the longer-term plan for instituting pay for performance for both the Senior Foreign Service and the Senior Executive Service," he says, "they've given us a lot of flexibility." In addition, the new personnel rules covering the Defense Department and the Department of Homeland Security, mentioned above, "are causing all of us to have to look at our civil service personnel systems, below the senior level, and see how they might evolve. And there again, I think OPM is giving people a chance to come up with their own ideas."

The Chief Human Capital Officers Act was in part a response to a potentially perilous workforce crisis in which an unusually large number of civil servants become eligible to retire or take early retirement between 2003 and 2005. That would leave a serious knowledge gap at the top of the government's permanent workforce. Replacing lost experience and talent at senior levels is never easy for any organization. The federal government, however, labors under special problems in personnel recruitment at all levels: the sheer size of its workforce, its inability at higher grade levels to match private sector salaries, and the disinclination to consider a government career that opinion polls detect in a majority of young people.

Also very much in this picture are government's entangled hiring procedures, as made clear by *Washington Post* columnist Stephen Barr in June 2004. He noted the several kinds of new flexibility in hiring granted to federal agencies by the 2002 legislation as well as the Office of Personnel Management's recent report that agencies were not yet using them. Government websites list 17,000 job openings on most days, Barr wrote, but applicants can run into many pages of instructions, requests for considerable supporting documentation, and questions to be answered. Most civil service experts agree, he said, "that the government's approach discourages people from seeking federal employment" and, when they do seek it, "often fails to identify the best-qualified applicants." He added that many applicants wait "six months to a year" before receiving a job offer and often get "little or no feedback" on the status of their applications.

"The key missing link in government transformation, and in achieving a more results-oriented government, has been the people element," U.S. Comptroller General David Walker says. "For too many years, the federal government treated its employees as a cost to be cut, rather than an asset to be appreciated. But when you're in a knowledge-based business, you're only as good as your people." With government representing 20 percent of the U.S. economy, "we can't afford anything less than first-rate people running it."

Walker makes another point on the people issue.

» We have to keep in mind that employees will behave based upon how they're measured. One of the things that I've found is that, while agencies might have strategic plans and even outcome-based measures, most do not have modern, effective, and credible performance-appraisal systems for their employees. They don't have systems that link how employees are getting evaluated, how they get paid, and the basis on which they get promoted. They're not linked to the desired outcomes for the institution.

Government must move faster and more broadly to develop these systems, "because when you do that, you can move organizations pretty quickly. You can achieve economies, efficiencies, and enhance effectiveness at a much more accelerated pace. But an overwhelming majority of federal government agencies haven't done that yet, and it's the key missing link."

The Chief Acquisition Officers Council

Until recently called the Federal Acquisition Council, this group changed its name following homeland security legislation enacted in 2002 that required agencies to appoint chief acquisition officers. Actually, according to David Safavian, chief of staff at the General Services Administration, the group began life as the Procurement Executives Council—originally a forum for "a bunch of procurement types to get together and chat away on what their problems were." The problem, says Safavian, was that membership in the Procurement Executives Council was limited to senior procurement executives, in effect excluding participants who might add value to the discussions. So his predecessor organized a Federal Acquisition Council, "made up not just of senior procurement executives, but [also] competitive sourcing officials and other management people who did have responsibility, at least in part, over acquisition issues." Rather than focusing on challenges in the acquisition process, Safavian recounts, the Federal Acquisition Council concentrated on the President's Management Agenda from the perspective of procurement matters. The reason was that "procurement really goes to the heart of a number of the President's Management Agenda items."

Since competitive sourcing is one of the five management agenda initiatives and, in Safavian's view, is really acquisition-based, the CAO Council started discussing competitive sourcing issues. The same is true of information technology issues, he says. "A lot of discussion in the Chief Information Officers Council is about what systems need to be purchased, and how." In addition to its competitive sourcing subcommittee, therefore, the CAO Council has an e-government subcommittee, to deal with technology issues. Similarly, other CAO Council subcommittees focus on human capital and financial management.

As a group bringing together federal acquisition professionals, the CAO Council offers a high-level forum to track and advance the federal acquisition system. It advocates business practices designed to make possible the on-time delivery of the best possible products and services to agencies while emphasizing integrity, fairness, competition, and openness in federal acquisitions. The council is led by the administrator of OMB's Office of Federal Procurement Policy and works closely with the Federal Acquisition Regulatory Council to promote sound business practices in the acquisition system.

The council convenes every two months. "We get an update from the subcommittees about the progress that they've made on, say, a best-practices guide, or a core competency list, a certification list, things like that," Safavian says. In addition, the council's subcommittees meet individually. Its membership of about thirty mixes career civil servants and appointees, and includes some agency inspectors general. Twenty-three major federal agencies are represented; small agencies have a representative as well.

As of June 2004, Safavian was awaiting Senate confirmation as the director of the Office of Federal Procurement Policy, and as such he would also lead the CAO Council. But in his present position at the General Services Administration, the government's chief support services and procurement agency, Safavian has strong views on the quality of the people who constitute the federal government's acquisition community. "Making sure we have the best-trained acquisition workforce that knows not just how to buy things quickly, but buy things well, is a fundamental function of government," he says. "It's not one that people focus on very often, but when they do, they tend to focus on it in a very bad way." What Safavian has consistently been promoting as a first priority, therefore, is improvement of the acquisition workforce—"better, more efficient training and a career development path."

He sees a role here for the CAO Council in setting standards, citing as an example the Defense Acquisition Workforce Improvement Act, which mandates standards for the Defense Department. Since the civilian federal acquisition community has no such requirement, the CAO Council is currently "taking a look at what tools we have, what arrows are in our quiver, to improve workforce training." Illustrating the urgency of that task is the contrast between the extensive training now offered military acquisition officials and the programs directed toward their far less numerous civilian colleagues. The Defense Acquisition University, according to Safavian's figures, "has five hundred people doing nothing but training and testing and developing materials for training, and a budget of $100 million. That's $100 million, five hundred people, for two-thirds of the acquisition workforce." At the Federal Acquisition Institute, on the other hand, there are "three full-time people and an $8 million budget." Safavian would like to merge the two, despite some inherent resistance on the civilian side. "Rather than reinvent the wheel, merely to protect the civilian side's turf, our hope is that we can get these two to work together. Buying an aircraft carrier is not that much different than buying a billion-dollar IT system, in terms of the acquisition principles. There are some more fundamental building-block concepts."

He believes the CAO Council will support the policy initiatives coming from the Office of Federal Procurement Policy. For new ideas, he says, the council is both a good sounding board for comment and a good research mechanism for identifying which issues need to be looked into.

CHAPTER 4

Leadership Positions

Three of the positions discussed in this chapter emerged from the extensive management reform undertaken by the executive and legislative branches in the 1990s. All of them connect directly and intimately to the mandates, organizations, and procedures at the center of federal management today. Just as important, they operate within the top echelons and at the core of federal departments and agencies. "That sends a very important signal to the public that we care about management," said John Koskinen, deputy director for management at the Office of Management and Budget (OMB) in the Clinton administration. "But it also helps the departments by providing management leadership at senior levels of the organization."

Chief Operating Officer

Even before their designation as "chief operating officers" (COOs) during the early 1990s, deputy secretaries and other top agency officers across the federal government were responsible for making their departments or agencies run on a daily basis, overseeing the execution of policy, mediating between conflicting interests, taking on special assignments. Not all chief operating officers are political appointees, nor are they necessarily their agencies' seconds in command. Those who are political appointees, however, have often also functioned as "clones" of their agency chiefs, ready to assume the top leadership and representational roles whenever the boss for whatever reason was elsewhere, committed to administration policy, normally able to connect when necessary to the political power centers of other agencies, the White House, OMB, and Congress. As members of the President's Management Council since 1993, agency COOs are decisionmakers with responsibilities for instituting government-wide management policy.

While most practitioners and observers agree on the necessity of the COO position, discussion has continued about the nature of the job and its scope, power, and rapport with the agency's chief. The question has arisen, for example, whether the deputy position is the right level for the COO function. Some veterans we interviewed for earlier Prune Books feel it doesn't matter as long as a senior agency official has the COO responsibility. "Someone needs to have it," said one, suggesting it could be given to the agency's chief of staff or the under secretary for management, or shared between the chief of staff and the deputy secretary. Others believe strongly (and, we believe, correctly) that the operating role of the COO cannot be separated from the political. "Nobody else could be the COO other than the deputy," a COO said. The political content of the COO job is important, said another. "To make decisions, to make them stick within the department, to be able to sell them on the Hill, you have to be part of the political team." Another said that without operational control at the top, individual decisions are the product of policy choices instead of "a longer-term sense of where those policies should be taking us."

A second question focuses on the relationship between the deputy secretary–COO and the head of the agency. According to widely endorsed conventional wisdom, no one should accept a deputy position without the full support of the agency head. That may not be possible if, as sometimes happens, the deputy is the choice of the White House instead of the person leading the agency. But if the result is a lack of full confidence or trust from the top, it can undermine a deputy's effectiveness and clout, whether as deputy or as COO. Innovations or improvements that a COO might want to make are impossible, a COO told us, unless the chief of the agency believes these changes are important.

That raises, in turn, the matter of a COO's relationship with the agency's chief of staff. One COO we have talked with viewed the chief of staff as "basically the secretary's political person." Another said some chiefs of staff "don't believe they work for anybody but the secretary." They variously advised COOs to correct such impressions, make certain that zones of influence are mutually understood, develop good relations with their agencies' chiefs of staff, avoid the appearance of diverse power centers, and use the prerogative of the job to be a decisionmaker.

What are typical COO activities? "I have authority over the day-to-day operations—finance, management, budget," says Eugene Hickok at the Department of Education. It's a little bit of everything:

» I meet weekly with the assistant secretaries who deal with the management end of the operation—information officer, finance officer, management and budget—and program assistant secretaries of special education, vocational education, elementary and secondary education. A handful of us meets every day as an executive leadership team—the secretary, chief counsel, and myself. From that hour on I have constant interactions with other offices, based on what the issue is. I have a lot of interaction with the Domestic Policy Council, more now than in the past, and the opportunity to brief the president periodically on the issues.

At the Treasury Department, Deputy Secretary and COO Samuel Bodman sees the job's functions as

» trying to respond to the budgetary responsibilities, to have adequate resources, to negotiate—first internally, then with the Office of Management and Budget, then with the Hill—to help secure the resources that we need to manage the department. It's to make sure we manage our financial affairs with integrity, transparency, and responsibility. That we have human resource programs, policies, and initiatives that will help us do the right thing by our people. And that we look after the physical facilities of this building and other buildings that house Treasury employees.

What credentials should a prospective COO bring to the job? "It's important to have at least some perspective on what the realities of the public sector are," says Mortimer Downey, a former COO and deputy secretary of the Department of Transportation. "Some people who have come in, who have totally grown up in the private sector, are often clueless."

The U.S. Comptroller General, David Walker, has a long perspective on the matter of qualifications at this level. He recognizes that part of the challenge of government is the large number of players that have to get involved in order to get things done. This makes it especially tough in trying to deal with the systemic and structural issues involved in achieving meaningful, durable change. The Department of Defense, for example, "is number one in the world in fighting and winning armed conflicts. But it is poor, at best, on economy, efficiency, transparency, and accountability." Part of the reason is lack of continuity within the department:

» They haven't had their top political leadership over the years really focused on the basic parts of management. And they haven't had people who have been there long enough to be able to deal with the long-standing problems. What it takes for any enterprise to operate economically, efficiently, effectively, no matter whether a Democrat or a Republican is in the White House, is to be there long enough to see things through. That doesn't exist right now.

The answer, Walker believes, is term appointments of professionals from the public or private sectors "who have performance contracts, report directly to agencies' top officials, and have a degree of continuity." They would focus full time on "strategic planning, organizational alignment, financial management, human capital strategy, information technology, knowledge management, change management." In other words, they would be career COOs whose terms could span administrations in order to address major management challenges on an ongoing basis and whose exclusive concern would be results-focused management. Their appointments would come in at executive level 2, Walker proposes, "meaning deputy secretary for management or principal under secretary for management."

Walker also notes that not all individuals appointed as deputy secretaries have significant experience as COOs or the time or interest to focus on management issues:

» In some cases—in fact, in most cases—deputy secretaries already have a pretty full plate of issues that don't have anything to do with basic management and the functions of a chief operating officer. In fact, many people come into government in those kinds of roles for the policy side of it, rather than the operations side. That's why we at GAO believe that a number of major departments and agencies actually need a level-2 appointment of the kind I'm talking about.

Chief Information Officer

In the 1980s and 1990s, the federal government experienced many large-scale failures in information technology. Persistent congressional questions produced a task force led by OMB to investigate the large cost overruns and delays typical of information technology projects among the agencies.

Legislation intended to correct the situation developed during the Clinton administration. The 1996 Information Technology Management Reform Act (popularly known as the Clinger-Cohen Act) called in part for increased control of agencies' investments in information technology to make these functions consistent with mission and to see whether the private sector could perform them more effectively at less cost. It conditioned investments in new technology on the redesign of systems, if necessary. The legislation told federal agencies to set up a comprehensive approach to the acquisition, use, and disposal of information technology and said information technology investments should support each agency's strategic operational goals and delivery of services to the public.

In the wake of Clinger-Cohen, all twenty-four major cabinet departments and executive agencies created chief information officer (CIO) positions. Driven by the anticipated computer programming crisis during the transition from 1999 to 2000, agencies also moved into information-management processes, such as controls on information technology investment, cost-estimation processes, and IT architecture, and put their CIOs in charge. Later, OMB created the Exhibit 300 Capital Asset Plan and Business Case procedure (see chapter 5), requiring agencies to report on and justify their major investments, including information technology, annually. To further improve federal management of information resources and support it with central direction and coordination, the E-Government Act of 2002 established an Office of Electronic Government and Information Technology within OMB. (To a significant degree, that provision responded to a recommendation in *E-Government: The Next American Revolution,* published in 2001 by the Council for Excellence in Government.)

The CIO position in a federal agency "is not a technology function," says Mark Forman, who was the e-government and information technology chief at OMB, 2001–03. "This is a business transformation function. That's why some companies don't use the term 'CIO.' CIOs are chief information officers, not chief information technology officers. You've got to know the technology, but at the end of the day you're responsible for inserting technology into business processes and information management."

Karen Evans, a former CIO at the Department of Energy who succeeded Forman at OMB, expresses a similar view. "An agency CIO is not just a technology specialist, but an important adviser to the agency head and the chief financial officer on agency business issues," she says. "The CIO helps set and oversees direction for an agency in utilizing and spending its IT investments." CIOs must develop an inclusive vision for the role of information technology investments in the overall success of agencies' missions and a "strong understanding of the personnel, procurement, hiring, and other processes" that contribute to reaching specific goals. Evans advises CIOs "to understand that they are solutions-providers to agency business leaders in achieving overall agency missions."

Information is the operative word here. The real-time exchange and use of information—government to citizens, government to business, government to government—is what electronic government is all about. It's easy to overstate e-government's unusual potential. The fact remains, however, that government carries a key responsibility to serve people and institutions, private and public, in ways that no other entity can. E-government, when more fully achieved, can make that task far more productive, more transparent, faster, and easier. For individuals or businesses, it can supply government information and services online that are cheaper, more accessible, and more accountable than the alternatives. For all levels of government in America, it can accelerate and ease the way in which they do business and communicate with one another. Most important, perhaps, e-government can tighten the connections between government and citizens, building understanding, confidence, and participation where too little now exists.

Only a few years ago, tough problems barred the path to those objectives. Agencies designed their information technology mostly to serve their own needs, not those of citizens. True, scores of federal websites with millions of pages were available to Americans. Some e-government did operate in areas like rule making, procurement, and weather information. But, amid all the information at their disposal, citizens found no one-stop, easy way to find what they specifically needed. Channels to engage with government were insufficient. The redundant, disconnected federal e-government structure contained three hundred existing or planned initiatives, but no overall strategy for consistent, coordinated operation and progress.

In 1998, the situation began to change. The Government Paperwork Elimination Act of that year directed the federal government to put all its services and transactions online by 2003. The Clinton administration followed with executive orders responding to that instruction. Subsequent legislation and a new mandate from the Bush administration picked up the pace. The first director of OMB's new Office of Electronic Government and Information Technology was charged under the President's Management Agenda to move toward an expanded, market-based e-government oriented to citizens and results. From those hundreds of e-government programs, OMB in the fall of 2001 chose twenty-four that offered the best early promise of cost-effective services to users and a range that extended across government over multiple agencies, and quickly pushed the programs toward maturity and greater productivity.

Among the best known of them is www.firstgov.gov, the official federal government web portal. Its users get fast access to all federal government transactions, services, and information, plus links to state and local governments. Structured by topics and audiences, reaching across agency lines, the site is designed to get users to their specific information or services targets in three mouse clicks. Another initiative, IRS Free File (www.irs.gov/efile), enables many taxpayers to file federal returns quickly, with return receipt acknowledgement and faster refunds; in the 2004 tax-filing season, this service expected 3.5 million users. Within the federal government, E-Payroll telescoped twenty-two federal payroll centers into two, with a reported saving of $1.2 billion in ten years. A fourth e-government program, E-gov (www.whitehouse.gov/omb/egov), updates users about the federal e-government effort itself.

Underlining the importance of these advances, U.S. Comptroller General David Walker also points to an issue that remains of concern both to those who design and operate e-government and the millions who use it. "We also have to make sure we do it," he warns, "in a way that is respectful of privacy and knowledgeable of security concerns that exist when you're dealing with an electronic environment."

CIO responsibilities are sometimes a part of larger portfolios. A case in point is the job of the assistant secretary for budget, technology, and finance at the Department of Health and Human Services. When we talked with him, Kerry Weems was the acting assistant secretary. Though he was the chief financial officer, his job also had oversight responsibilities for information technology; his department financially supports the government-wide e-government initiatives that are germane to it, and some of his employees have worked on them. "I think they've chosen the e-government initiatives wisely," he says. "A lot of those projects make sense. That's why I think they'll be successful. And that's also the reason that the next step in e-government that OMB is talking about now are the lines of business, where they're looking even more broadly across government, and saying, 'OK, what if we had a single standard for a financial system?'"

At the Defense Department, CIO responsibilities have always resided in the area formerly called C3I—command, control, communications, and intelligence. In 2003, the intelligence activities of the office were split off and lodged with the under secretary of defense (intelligence). The remaining C3 functions are today the responsibility of the assistant secretary of defense for network and information integration and the CIO, who at this writing was Linton Wells II in an acting capacity. No one could argue that his job is typical of CIO positions elsewhere in government. But it does provide an idea of the functional range and workload that federal CIOs can be asked to handle, particularly as technology's role continues to expand. Wells says his position and organization were renamed to better define "the kind of transformational assignment that we have." His office's website describes that assignment as to "lead the information age transformation of the department by building the foundation for network-centric operations through policies, program oversight, resource allocation, and the provision of value-added support."

In other words, Wells says, the department "is transforming to a network-centric environment. We're moving from a department in which each ship, tank, and plane was an independent entity, to where they are now nodes on a broad network that ties together both the war-fighting and business practices, enabling access to information to perform our mission." The basic model here is "better shared situational awareness of what's going on" across the department. "The key contributor to that is to build this information-sharing environment. That's one of the large functions we have."

Five major programs contribute to the network. One of them is the Joint Tactical Radio System, which is a software-controllable radio. Whereas a single person must now haul three to five radios around in order to communicate in a battle situation, the new software in the radio makes it possible to build several functions into a single piece of portable hardware. At one moment, given proper antennae and auxiliary equipment, it might be communicating with someone in view of the user; at another, it could be talking via satellite. The utility of this radio system, however, ranges beyond the military and across government to provide new and urgently required capability. In emergencies, for example, it will permit the military to interact with state and local first-responders. "Right now, when we operate on our fixed frequency bands, the military radios are prohibited from being in the same frequency bands as the police and fire," Wells says. "This will now let us interoperate better with them. We've got a lot of work going on with Homeland Security in terms of more closely integrating our network."

Wells, who has been "involved in various parts of the national security and emergency preparedness business since the mid-1990s," is a member of a group called the Committee of Principals for the National Communications System. "It is primarily intended to provide emergency preparedness communications for the country," he says, and it links elements of the Department of Homeland Security with other agencies with related concerns. The Committee of Principals is designed to sort and solve a variety of crisis-related communications problems. "There are a lot of policy issues in sharing information," Wells points out. "For example, most mayors and police chiefs and fire chiefs don't have classified clearances. But a lot of the intelligence information that comes in is classified. How do you find ways to sanitize that information in national security situations so you can share it with the state and local first-responders?"

The National Communications System sponsors the National Security Telecommunications Advisory Committee to the President, or NSTAC, which supplies industry-based recommendations to the president on national security telecommunications policy. In addition to thirty senior executives of the largest telecommunications firms in the country, this group includes twenty-two federal agencies in its membership, the executive office of the president, and the secretary of defense. Dating from 1982, the NSTAC also serves as a forum for industry-government planning. "So, in essence," Wells says, "our interaction in the interagency and the emergency preparedness community is through the Committee of Principals, and with the private sector it is through the NSTAC."

The Defense Department's annual information technology budget, which Wells's office oversees, is about $28 billion. His advice to CIOs working with OMB is to "have your ducks in a row when you go over there. Too often, we've gone over and sort of said, 'Information technology is good; give us more money.'" That's probably a forgivable instinct, given the information revolution, the money being made from information technology, and vendors promoting its transformational nature. But, Wells says

» OMB has been pretty good about holding our feet to the fire and saying, "Come back and justify it, tell us what you're doing." Occasionally, it's been frustrating. Some of the models for business cases [the OMB Exhibit 300 process, outlined in chapter 5] don't always translate into the national security system. It's kind of hard to figure out an economic return on an aircraft carrier. But we've had a good relationship with OMB, and we certainly applaud the various e-government initiatives. E-authentication is the one in which we participate most vigorously.

On the qualifications for his position, Wells says that network and information integration "works two sides. One is communications, and the other is information. The skills you need actually to manage a network with information flows in it are rather different from what you need to build radios and communication satellites and things like that. But generally, a strong industrial background in either the information technology era or the telecommunications industry would be a good mix for this job." Wells's own background lies mostly in technology and policy. "It's amazing how many people in policy are not comfortable with numbers and technological issues," he observes, "and how many who work the engineering sides don't think of the policy context in which their work takes place. But telecommunications is more than just a techie issue. It is a core strategic advantage of the United States."

With that in mind, note the counsel that Mark Forman would give newly appointed CIOs: "One, understand the business processes, the performance measures for those processes, throughout the agency. Two, identify the highest priority, mission-critical gaps in agency performance. Three, partner with the people who have the biggest gaps and become a problem solver through the use of redesigned business processes, integration, and the use of IT to close those performance gaps."

Chief Financial Officer

In 1990, the Chief Financial Officers Act envisaged comprehensive reform of federal financial management. It created a new leadership structure at OMB, instituted long-range planning, required audited financial statements, and held each agency to stronger accountability. It established twenty-plus chief financial officer (CFO) positions at principal agencies and tasked them with developing and managing a number of agency functions. Among these were integrated accounting and financial management systems, policy guidance and oversight of financial management personnel and operations, design of financial management systems, and cash and credit management. The legislation was not explicit on which of a variety of agency financial operations, such as budget preparation, should be subject to the oversight of the CFO. OMB directives on the functions that CFOs should supervise were equally unspecific; that was left to individual agencies. The result is a somewhat mixed pattern of CFO duties from agency to agency.

"You don't need to be an accountant to be in this job," says CFO Christopher Burnham at the Department of State. "While I think it probably helped four years ago when the job was just the chief financial officer and not the assistant secretary for resource management, this is now more of a management and leadership job. And while I think it's very important to have a strong financial background, it's more important that you have a demonstrated management and leadership background." For Burnham, the job is comparable with that of the CFO in a large corporation. CFOs are "critical senior members" of any corporate team, setting the strategy for ensuring return on equity and earnings per share, digging out waste, "constantly figuring out how to do things like recapitalize the company, maximize acquisitions, or spin off subsidiaries" that no longer match the strategic vision of the corporation. "That is really the role of the modern corporate CFO, and it should be the role of a modern government CFO."

But a solid understanding of finance is important, developed either in government finance, corporate finance, or both. "It could be the perspective of someone from Capitol Hill or from OMB or from General Electric or from Hewlett Packard," Burnham says. "Someone who has run something, maybe even fixed something, bought something, bought a company and figured out how to make that work in the confines of integrating it into a larger enterprise, a team builder." Managing the huge volume of information coming in all the time is impossible without a competent team. Delegation is therefore an important aspect of the job.

At the Department of Health and Human Services, we asked acting Assistant Secretary for Budget, Technology, and Finance Kerry Weems what kind of background best qualifies an individual for a chief financial officer position. Weems, a career official who is also the agency's CFO, "would look for a generalist, somebody who has a lot of energy and can take the long view, somebody who's patient. This is not a job for impatience." Specific skills in financial management or in information technology (where Weems also has oversight) are not really required. "My career staff can offer any political person, in terms of knowledge, anything they want in these areas," he says—experts in budget, experts in finance, experts in IT. The job doesn't need an expert in those areas, he says; it needs "a leader in those areas. That's what is expected of the political leadership that comes in."

Because budget is the largest part of the portfolio, in terms of time and perhaps political importance, Weems says, often someone is chosen for the job who "they think has had budget experience. The problem with that is, many times they're from the Hill, and have had some budget experience. Almost everybody on the Hill gets to touch a budget somewhere at some time, but it doesn't make them an expert. I would prefer, actually, somebody who would come here and say, 'I'm not an expert.'"

Weems works in an agency that by many measures is the federal government's largest. But the variety of his duties shows what Christopher Burnham at the State Department means by the "modern government CFO" and is instructive for CFOs everywhere in government. Weems spends most of his time on budget matters, including working with congressional appropriators:

» I think probably the hardest part of my job right now is, nobody likes the budget as it comes out. Everybody has to live with it, but they don't like it. So there's always some effort to rearrange the budget. I do my best to accommodate them, but that is very hard. Because a budget, being a policy document, is also many times a product of many compromises. Pull one string, and the whole thing starts to unravel.

Information technology is another principal responsibility of Weems's job. The secretary of Health and Human Services, for example, has asked for significant changes. "He's asked me, 'Why do we have seventeen e-mail systems? I want only one. Why does every [sub] agency have multiple contracts to support its services contracts? I want one. Why are there eight different networks? I want one.'" With the department chief information officer, who works for him, Weems has put in time to undertake those changes.

» And bit by bit, we have succeeded. The precedent condition for a lot of those things is now in place. That is, the department is now on a unitary network. There's a contract in place that'll put us on a single e-mail system by the end of this fiscal year. We have reduced the number of service contracts from a very large number to about seven. We're going to have unitary buys of PCs—commodity PC buys, not special applications.

Weems says the next planned step goes beyond infrastructure into planning and portfolio management for updated information technology applications that the department's subagencies need. Examples are a surveillance system for the Centers for Disease Control and Prevention or a food-safety system for the Food and Drug Administration. "This is one of the places where the IT world very closely touches the budget world and the performance outcomes world," he says. "How much does it cost? Does it really give us the performance outcomes we're looking for?" In the budget world, information technology was once "something you bought by the yard." But there wasn't much belief that the department's component agencies could show "how the IT that we were buying was connected to program outcomes. We expect to be able to do that."

At the State Department, CFO Burnham also deals with the technology challenge. "We're running an incredibly complicated global organization in over 130 currencies, every time zone, in all but just a handful of countries," he points out. "How do we get everybody using the same accounting system, or the same voucher system, or accounting for real property the same way?" The answer was to throw out the old legacy accounting and disbursing systems. "We had to transition into one global financial platform using a commercial, off-the-shelf product; again, at over 250 locations around the world in 170 countries. Now we have to make sure we have second-to-second connectivity via the Internet, something we couldn't do as recently as three years ago because of bandwidth limitations or bandwidth costs."

In an agency that operates at multiple locations throughout the world with a workforce of 25,000 employees, both American and foreign, on a budget of $30 billion, part of Burnham's task is "to bring in performance metrics" on goals as hard to pin down as helping build democracy or prosperity or trying to lower HIV infection rates. Some of them are almost impossible to measure. But again, Burnham is talking about the desired approach of any federal CFO when he says,

» we are imposing upon ourselves the same principles on which we run a business in the private sector—responsibility to our shareholders, careful stewardship, and fiduciary responsibility with the funds entrusted to us, and making sure that we're earning some return. [He calls it] return on effort—that's what I'm trying to measure. To simplify, it can be difficult to get government to think along business-plan lines.

Weems at the Department of Health and Human Services (HHS) believes that shortening the auditing period between the closing of federal agencies' books for the fiscal year and the date when audited financial statements are due has posed a particular challenge in his job. In 2005, that time span will drop from five months to forty-five days. Telescoping the auditing process, says Weems, is "a very, very big deal. Most of my energies in that particular role are devoted to maintaining the clean audit opinion [Weems's department was one of the first to earn one], working with the auditors, and managing the changes that we've had to make in the audit over the last couple of years, mainly to deal with accelerating it."

All agencies with CFOs produce audited financial statements each year (before passage of the CFO Act of 1990, only two did). Ideally, the audit of a financial statement generates a clean opinion: the audit finds that all information stated by the agency is in order, accurate, and straightforward in all substantive matters. David Walker of the GAO recalls that people once defined success in federal financial management by "whether you got a clean opinion on your financial statements." Thousands of hours and millions of dollars were consumed, he says, in "re-creating the books after the end of the year, so that their auditors could give them a clean opinion five months later. Not only is that not success in financial management, that's waste."

Early in the George W. Bush administration, he says, the GAO reached agreement with OMB and the Treasury Department on the definition of success. It's a combination of four factors that are, in Walker's words: "a clean opinion on your financial statements, no material internal-control weaknesses, no major compliance problems, and systems that provide for timely, accurate, and useful financial and management information, to make informed decisions on a day-to-day basis."

Before those criteria took effect, Walker recalls, twenty of twenty-four major agencies were judged to be successful. After, the number dropped to three. "But I would argue that is substantive success." Moreover, the new short audit period will rule out reinventing the books after the end of the year. Walker suggests that the same effort can now be invested "on getting the systems right, on trying to make sure they've got the controls in place, on trying to make sure that they've got issues addressed up front. Which is the right way to do it."

At HHS, CFO Weems said that despite his agency's size and complexity, it was able to produce its most recent audited financial statements in something approximating forty-five days "and kept our clean opinion in so doing." That success was achieved "by setting clear strategic goals and leaving the details to the people who are actually responsible for carrying this out"—the deputy CFO and the CFOs in each of the department's subagencies—"and demanding that they work together in a collaborative fashion. Because we don't do individual unit audits anymore, we do a unitary audit for [the department]. So that means that everybody has to cooperate to be able to pull this off in a timely way."

As is the case with most of the other positions discussed in this chapter, the quality of the workforce supporting the function is a continuing concern. In a 2000 survey of agency CFOs and deputy CFOs serving in the Clinton administration, for example, PricewaterhouseCoopers partner Steve Watson and consultant Kent Owens found that concern "perhaps the most pressing issue" discussed. CFOs they interviewed worried about being able to find and keep competent financial and information technology professionals. With an eye on the future, one of them, Department of Labor CFO Kenneth Bresnahan, said the problem had to be addressed quickly, "as many financial managers are eligible to retire in the next five years."*

Inspector General

Fraud, waste, and abuse are an old catchall for the variety of wrongdoing in government. Matched against that threesome is another: audit, inspect, and investigate. In more than fifty agencies and subagencies, those actions describe the mandate of the inspector general. But as a former inspector general puts it, "Any damned fool can find fraud, waste, and abuse. Preventing it is what takes brains." That's why Clark Kent Ervin, inspector general at the Department of Homeland Security, takes pains to characterize the job as anything but a "gotcha" operation. "It's our job," he says, "to examine thoroughly the programs and operations of the departments for which we have oversight responsibility and give the departments due credit for those areas where we think they're doing well, those areas where the departments are making progress." It is equally his office's responsibility to be critical where the Department of Homeland Security or one of its agencies is not doing well and room for improvement exists.

Ervin stresses the need to "understand the nature of the job and the attributes required to do it effectively." Assertiveness and aggressiveness are important, but so are objectivity and neutrality in evaluating programs and operations. Given human nature, Ervin says, most program managers don't take easily to criticism of what they are doing. So "it is incumbent on us to go about our work in as constructive and positive manner as possible—being as diplomatic as possible, and keeping in mind that at the end of the day our power is hortatory. We can only recommend things. It's up to the department managers as to whether they agree to implement our recom-

*From "Changing Organizations: The Chief Financial Officer Act—10 Years Later," in *The Business of Government* (PricewaterhouseCoopers Endowment for the Business of Government [now the IBM Center for the Business of Government], Spring 2000).

mendations." He wants his operation to be seen as a constructive influence, "to be consulted early and often, as opposed to waiting until we've issued a report that might in the end be critical." An inspector general operation should avoid gratuitous criticism and point out solutions, not just problems. "We try to be as flexible as we can to craft an alternative when the department agrees with the intent of a recommendation but doesn't want to implement it in exactly the way that we would."

June Gibbs Brown served as inspector general at HHS during the Clinton administration. "If you really can work in sync" with an agency's leadership, she told us for an earlier Prune Book, "and they have an appreciation for what you're doing, they are going to use the products you produce, and you will be more effective. If they don't respect your office and what you're producing, you may as well forget it, because you're not going to get changes as the result of your work."

The federal inspector general position emerged in the 1960s at the Department of Agriculture, and inspectors general operated in the 1970s at the Department of Housing and Urban Development and the old Department of Health, Education, and Welfare. The audit, inspection, and investigatory functions that had developed to that point, however, were fragmented and isolated from one another. Most of all, the inspector general function lacked statutory standing, authority, and independence. In 1976, over the opposition of OMB and most agencies, the Congress created a statutory inspector general at Health, Education, and Welfare, appointed by the president. Backers of the statutory inspector general concept later added a dozen more agencies and succeeded in 1978 in adding an expanded inspector general bill as a rider on other legislation. Its backers left the Defense Department out of the enacted bill because of the risk that Pentagon opposition would doom it; later, they brought the Pentagon in.

Eventually, via the 1978 Inspector General Act and subsequent legislation, particularly amendments in 1988, more than fifty independent inspector general offices were established at cabinet departments, independent agencies, and other "designated federal entities." Thirty-three inspectors general were to be appointed by the heads of their organizations; the rest were presidential appointees, reporting to the heads of their agencies but removable only by the president. All had the same authority and responsibilities. Given subpoena powers, they were tasked with auditing and inspecting the activities of their agencies and making recommendations to management that would increase the efficiency and impact of programs and lower their cost.

The 1978 legislation directed agency inspectors general to report twice a year to their agency chiefs and Congress about activities in the prior six months. Their reports were to describe major problems, corrective recommendations, and previous recommendations not acted on and to list cases sent for prosecution, the results of these, and audit and other reports made since the last report. As of 1988, in addition, the agencies were required to report to Congress twice a year on how they responded to their IGs' recommendations. In 1990, the Chief Financial Officers Act assigned inspectors general the job of auditing their agencies' financial statements annually. Further responsibilities came with the Paperwork Reduction Act and Clinger-Cohen legislation of the mid-1990s, extending the IG role into government's efforts to take fuller advantage of resources like information technology.

Inspectors general are alone among federal officials in departments and agencies who don't need clearance from OMB to communicate officially and formally with Congress. Their budgets are separate line items in their agencies' budget requests; their personnel authority is their own.

At the Department of Homeland Security, the Office of the Inspector General is an amalgam of staff from many of the twenty-two agencies the department has absorbed. Ervin, who oversees more than five hundred employees and a budget of $80 billion, points out that his office does program as well as financial auditing. "For example, my auditors recently completed what we call 'penetration testing': undercover teams have gone into various airports around the country to see whether they could penetrate the security systems, whether they could get guns, knives, and improvised bombs through the screening system there. That had nothing to do with finances."

On inspections: "There are a number of strictures laid out in something called the Yellow Book, promulgated by the Government Accountability Office, which require very laborious fact-checking and validation procedures. It's very good discipline to make sure the reports have integrity and are factually sound, but the process takes some time." Because auditors have to go through those strictures, he says, the inspections unit is valuable for "hot-button topics that the secretary and other senior managers, or the press, or Congress is interested in." He illustrates this with the requirement for criminal background checks for airport screeners. "A number of them had been hired without those checks done. Our inspections unit did it in a few weeks. The auditors just couldn't do that, because they've got to do these validation procedures."

On investigations: The inspector general's cadre of criminal investigators look into alleged criminal and serious noncriminal wrongdoing by department employees, contractors, and grantees. "That's a big, big job here because it's such a big department, 180,000 employees, and it's a huge grant-giving and contract-letting organization as well. The potential for wrongdoing, including criminal wrongdoing, is very big."

Ervin believes the pressure and conflict encountered by inspector general operations is exceptional:

» No one else's job is to criticize the department. We have the freedom to criticize when we think we need to, and we are unique because we're within the department but not of it. I report to the secretary but not in the way everybody else does. An IG can be removed only by the president and then the president must explain his reasons to Congress. That's intended to give the IG the independence to criticize the department when we think it's warranted.

He adds that his office has separate personnel, contracting, and budgetary authority, and separate legal counsel, "all designed to give us independence to do the job. That makes for difficulty. Sometimes the department cooperates and sometimes it doesn't. It requires a lot of diplomacy to be effective."

Similarities among federal inspector general positions abound, but so do differences. It is one set of circumstances, for instance, to function as an inspector general in an agency with big procurement and contracting operations; another if the agency makes grants or provides benefits; and yet another if the agency employs professional scientists, some of whom may be on the inspector general's own staff. Describing these differences, an inspector general once said, "If you've seen one IG's office, you've seen one IG's office."

To be effective, an inspector general needs technical competence, in Ervin's view, "which means, as the statute requires, expertise in one of the areas that's germane: law, accounting, management. Of those, the most important is management. We have lawyers. We have accountants. We have managers, but the inspector general is the ultimate general manager."

Chief Human Capital Officer

The Chief Human Capital Officers Act, contained in the 2002 Homeland Security legislation, took effect in 2003. It required every major federal agency to establish a chief human capital officer position, a job that addresses—at the working level—government's exceptionally important task of managing its people to best advantage.

In official language, a chief human capital officer is responsible for assembling, training, and managing a quality workforce; seeing to its strategic alignment with the agency's mission; and overseeing workforce policies and programs. The job is part of the agency's senior leadership. It has responsibility to the agency head for advice and assistance in selecting, training, and administering a high-quality, productive workforce in accordance with merit system principles.

It's a fair guess that this position faces more complexity at the Department of Homeland Security than at any other federal agency. As noted in the discussion of the Chief Human Capital Officers Council in chapter 3, the department is exempt from hiring, pay, and other civil service regulations; the fast-advancing uses of information technology present a special challenge for workforce management. Asa Hutchinson, the department's under secretary for border and transportation security, makes the technology point clear. "Our strategy is utilization of technology, and not just simply human resources," he explains. "Technology is a moving capability, an increasing capability. So when it comes to long-term human capital, you've got to look at how technology is going to change that investment." Currently, the Transportation Security Administration fields 45,000 airport screeners. What will that need be in the future? "You're going to have to grow with the industry, with airports adding screening checkpoints and new terminals. But then you're going to have technology that will improve the capability, perhaps reduce some of the lines of people year by year. Our challenge is to plan in terms of growth, but also in terms of technology, and carefully measure exactly what the human capital component will have to be."

The best human resources manager in the business, of course, can face a situation in which an operation needs more people but lacks the funds to hire them. At the Department of Health and Human Services, Assistant Secretary for Children and Families Wade Horn says this amounts, in effect, to downsizing. "As our number of programs grows and the amount of dollars that we oversee grows, we have less people to do the work. What's happening is that people retire, or people leave, and we don't have [funds] to replace them." Horn points out that his senior human resources person "doesn't control my budget. Congress does. It's not like I can go to the human resources person and say, 'Now, come on, go to your money tree in the back yard to get some more money so I can hire people.' That person has no greater capacity to overspend my budget than I do." That is a fundamental difference between the public sector and the private sector, he says, adding that a lot of political appointees don't perceive the distinction "and it takes them a while to really get it." Managers under his supervision regularly tell him they want to hire additional staff.

» I always have to explain that if I overspend my budget, I actually am guilty of a felony under the Anti-Deficiency Act. And I can't do that. I won't allow myself to be in a position where at the end of the year, I've got to furlough people because I've run out of money. It's not that I don't want to let them hire two or three new people, because five people have left, but because I've got to operate within a finite budget.

How does Horn handle such a problem? "Part of the way that you manage in a shrinking workforce is to make certain assumptions about how many people will leave. It's not until that assumption is proven wrong—that more people are leaving than you anticipated—that you're able to start to replace people." So far, his office hasn't reached that point and has been able to manage. "I think part of it is by increasing productivity. But also because, and this is sometimes a surprise to political appointees, there are really a lot of dedicated career employees in the federal bureaucracy."

At the Department of State, Director General of the Foreign Service Robert Pearson lists three personnel responsibilities, or goals, that he set after conversations with employees in Washington and overseas. First, consolidate the progress achieved in answering such fundamental workforce questions as "What are these people going to do? What are their careers going to be like? What quality of training and achievement do we expect them to have over the period of a career, both specialists and generalists?" Second, "create a stronger sense of partnership between the foreign service and the civil service in this building, and include our foreign employees overseas. We have almost 30,000 people overseas who work for us who are nationals of other countries, whether directly hired by us or working through contractors. Making these three segments a community is one of my priorities." Third is "a service that represents America. We are doing a number of things in marketing, recruiting, targeting, reexamining our examination process, in order to improve our recruitment and retention of minorities." Pearson says his job is "not one where the incumbent really is free to say what he or she wants to do. This job is about listening to what the collective thinks is important and trying to find a way to make it work."

The worldwide nature of his department's work poses some special issues for Pearson and means that he spends 40 percent of his time in cross-agency and Chief Human Capital Officers Council activities. In dealing with embassy staffing issues, for instance, he must take into account not only State's own employees. Numerous other federal agencies also operate overseas—Pearson remembers forty-eight during his time at the embassy in Paris, "everything from the Secret Service to NASA. We have to ensure that all those offices are correctly staffed." He regularly confronts problems connected to "somebody's presence in an embassy. How other agencies treat their family members somewhere, as opposed to how we treat our family members somewhere. All of those require attention."

Most of Pearson's annual budget of $220 million is spent on "moving our people back and forth around the world." On average, a third of the department's 10,000 foreign service generalists and specialists change location every year. "And that's their families, too, and all that goes with it, schooling, medical support, and the like." Almost 30,000 foreign employees work in American embassies and other missions abroad. "One of my offices is, in effect, the [Office of Personnel Management] for all of the foreign nationals who work for the State Department," Pearson says.

» It sets the policies and addresses their issues. Like any other entity in a foreign country, we are required to obey the labor laws of that country. So, for example, in countries that don't have an adequate retirement system for local employees, we have created a program in which employees can pay into a retirement fund. And we will provide their retirement, at the end of their service to the U.S. in those countries. Boutique solutions are required for lots of places.

CHAPTER 5

Management Support Structures

As senior leaders of government, presidential appointees should understand not just the ongoing effort to turn the federal government into a citizen-centered, results-focused institution or the processes and job missions that are the current vehicles of that effort. They must also be familiar with at least the major designs and structures recently developed to support the effort—even if they are unlikely to be engaged with them on a daily basis. This chapter outlines three such structural aids.

Why weren't these particular approaches attempted in earlier eras? Aren't greater coordination and less redundancy obvious answers to management and program inefficiency? At the beginning of this book, we traced the long history of attempts at reform; it isn't as if none of them recognized basic problems and envisioned appropriate solutions. But over those 50-plus years, the size of government has grown, its responsibilities, components, and costs have multiplied; and agencies, missions, and jobs have mutated, disappeared, reappeared, or merged under the impact of newly perceived needs, budget constraints, and reorganization. In the executive branch and Congress alike, all this has strengthened the natural inertia and resistance to change or loss of turf typical of large institutions. Against that background, reform of management is a drawn-out cycle of trial and measured progress.

Federal Enterprise Architecture

Since 2002, the Office of Management and Budget—OMB—has been putting in place a new mechanism intended to streamline and simplify the process of government. The Federal Enterprise Architecture, or FEA, is a business- and performance-based framework for a government centered on citizens and designed to get improved results through interagency collaboration.

The FEA rests on five interrelated "reference models" intended to smooth the progress of cross-agency analysis, correct duplicative investments, spot gaps, and find opportunities for collaboration within and across the federal establishment. Agencies that need access to initiatives aligned to the FEA and its associated reference models use the web-based Federal Enterprise Architecture Management System, which offers numerous ways for users to locate components, business services, and capabilities across the federal government.

The five models are the following:

—Business model: based on function, it avoids the use of older, stove-piped frameworks centered on agencies, unlike various other models that describe government with devices like organization charts or location maps.

—Performance model: an aggregate description of the data and information that support government programs and lines of business. It helps depict the types of interaction between the federal government and its customers, stakeholders, and business partners.

—Service component model: locates reusable software applications and services in the areas of process automation, business management, transactions, and customer service that agencies across government can apply.

—Data and information model: describes facts and statistics used in the interactions and exchanges that support government-wide program and business line operations.

—Technical model (completed in 2004): identifies standards, specifications, and technologies that support and enable the delivery of service components and capabilities.

The FEA seeks to implement the goals of the President's Management Agenda. With transparency and realism, it shows government's programs and business patterns as they exist and defines the improvements they can potentially achieve. It offers what have been called unprecedented opportunities to get rid of overlap, redundancy, and waste in the interactive matrix of citizens, businesses, government employees, and government. A typical target of this process is requirements that businesses submit nearly identical information to the federal government through a variety of channels with varying formats and efficiency. Another is more than a score of major federal payroll systems that perform the same basic service with widely varying per-transaction costs.

The promising results so far of the FEA can be credited to OMB leadership and government-industry partnership. But the work of the FEA remains far from complete. As viewed by David McClure, vice president for e-government and technology of the Council for Excellence in Government, the FEA process faces three main challenges. Testifying in May 2004 to the House Government Reform Subcommittee on Technology, he listed these challenges as (1) "ensuring disciplined agency architecture maturity and alignment," (2) "concentrating on tangible outcomes and measures of impact," and (3) "providing continuous, focused leadership." Yet putting agency-specific enterprise architectures in place falls short of "the true transformation [these architectures] can help create," McClure told the subcommittee. That transformation means "vertical alignment within agency boundaries and horizontal alignment across common functions and business processes of government." Although measuring compliance with proven methodologies and approaches is one valuable, necessary way of knowing whether processes are maturing, "it isn't enough by itself." Other measures of return—"demonstrating productivity gains, cost improvements in the delivery of information technology, cost savings from systems consolidation and component or application reuse"—are equally important.

Most important, McClure said, are the returns "that measure impact on direct mission-related performance." Well-constructed architectures should produce "visible changes" in program or service delivery outcomes. If the Department of Homeland Security's enterprise architecture enables it to recognize threats in minutes instead of days, real change has occurred. The same is true if a company can submit the same regulatory compliance information to government just once, online, instead of many times in many formats. Such an easing of the reporting burden lowers the company's administrative costs and raises its internal productivity. Other examples abound: a social security claim is resolved in hours or days because improvements in people, process, and technology minimize unnecessary data collection and get the right information to the right people quickly and reliably. With that, McClure said, "we have truly achieved a real return on investment." In particular, he pointed out, "enterprise architecture work requires leadership and executive understanding, commitment, participation, and constant attention." This can't be left solely to chief information officers. "The front pieces of the

Business Reference Model, the Performance Reference Model, and the Service Delivery Models have to be co-led by the business or program divisions," and "governance structures and decision processes must be in place to make this a reality."

Lines of Business

Building on the Federal Enterprise Architecture program, OMB, with the help of agency task forces, began in March 2004 to design what it calls "business-driven, common solutions" for five government-wide lines of business. Intended to support the objective (set out in the President's Management Agenda) of expanding electronic government, this methodology aims at allowing agencies to cut the cost of government by making business-performance improvements that share common architectures.

As defined by OMB, the five lines are financial management, health programs, and the management of human resources, grants, and litigation. Each is assigned an agency lead. For financial management, it is the Departments of Energy and Labor; for human resources, the Office of Personnel Management; for grants, the National Science Foundation and the Department of Education; for health, the Department of Health and Human Services; and for cases, the Department of Justice.

At the beginning of the effort, OMB's e-government administrator, Karen Evans, said that examination of Federal Enterprise Architecture data provided by agencies revealed "the need to review our planned investments in these five areas." All five lines share the same core business requirements and processes—duplication that doesn't fit with the current era of fiscal urgency and technological advance. At the same time, as OMB points out, each differs in the opportunities it presents and the effort necessary to reduce duplication and administrative workloads, save money, and speed up "significantly improved" delivery of services to citizens. OMB expects the lines-of-business undertaking to focus first on priorities that can achieve cost savings in fiscal 2005. By fall 2004, the agency teams were required to report in with "common solutions and a target architecture in business cases" that will be submitted to the budget review process and carried out in fiscal year 2006. Savings would then rise in fiscal 2006 as agencies move into common solutions. The effort would reach its major goals in fiscal 2007. Here is how OMB envisions the goals for each line of business:

—An efficient cross-government financial management solution that boosts business performance while guaranteeing integrity in accountability, financial controls, and the effectiveness of agency missions.

—Modern, cost-effective, standardized, integrated human resource information systems that support the strategic management of the workforce.

—A government-wide, comprehensive, integrated grants management system that ensures citizen access, customer service, and financial and technical stewardship.

—Citizens who are safer and healthier as the result of improved access to health-related information and services.

—Case management information that is easily and correctly shared within and among federal and local agencies and with citizens.

Exhibit 300 Capital Asset Plan and Business Case

This procedure for planning, budgeting, acquisition, and management of federal capital assets is a data-reporting vehicle. It sets out budget justification and reporting requirements that federal agencies must submit annually for new and ongoing major acquisitions and major information technology systems or projects included in their capital asset portfolios. Capital assets are land, structure, equipment, intellectual property, and information technology used by the federal government that have an estimated useful life of two years or more.

Underlying the thrust of the Exhibit 300 requirement is the axiom that if public funds are to be intelligently invested, the federal government has to handle its capital assets efficiently. Capital programming directly connects mission needs and capital assets. It combines the planning, acquisition, and management of capital assets with rigorous budget decisionmaking. The goal is to allow agencies to manage their assets to reach performance objectives with what OMB calls "minimal risk, lowest life-cycle costs, and greatest benefits to the agency's business." It also helps them obey the results-linked directives of a range of legislation.

There are two elements of the Exhibit 300 process, each aimed at gathering data used by OMB during budget review. An agency reviews its portfolio of capital assets to see whether it continues to meet mission requirements consistent with existing priorities, capabilities, and resources.

Capital asset investments are compared with one another, using criteria such as investment size, complexity, and expected improvements of performance. Thus rated and ranked, the investments form a prioritized portfolio.

According to OMB, the information an agency reports through the Exhibit 300 process helps OMB to:

—Understand the agency's capital programming and investment decisionmaking processes.

—Ensure that spending on capital assets directly supports the agency's mission and will provide a return on investment equal to or better than alternate uses of funding.

—Identify poorly performing projects: projects that are behind schedule, over budget, or not working.

—Identify capital assets that no longer fulfill ongoing or anticipated mission requirements or do not deliver intended benefits to the agency or its customers.

—Make certain that strong cases are made for investments in information technology; that these investments address security, privacy, and enterprise architecture and satisfy the effectiveness and efficiency gains planned by the business lines and functional operations.

PART THREE

CHAPTER 6

Prune Books, Past and Future

JOHN H. TRATTNER WITH FRANK A. WEIL

After six editions in the Prune Book series over a dozen years, we thought it was time in 2004 for the Council for Excellence in Government to ask some questions about Prune Books and to publish its findings. True, a considerable amount of anecdotal evidence and media attention has accumulated over the years. But it was clear that broader and more conclusive information was a necessary reality check. If only for planning purposes, we needed some answers. Should the Council continue publishing the book? If so, how can it be improved? What's valuable or useful about the series?

How the Council went about this, and the results obtained, are discussed further on. First, however, an assessment of this kind gains perspective with a brief review of the Prune Book's origins and its track record, particularly for readers who are unaware of them.

Background

The decision to launch the book began to take shape in the mid-1980s. In those days, just about the only organized information resource available to people seeking political appointment to senior federal positions was a congressional publication called *U.S. Government Policy and Supporting Positions*. It appeared at the time of each presidential election, issued alternatively by the Senate Governmental Affairs Committee and the House Committee on Government Reform and Oversight (and its variously named predecessors). Popularly known as the Plum Book, the publication was—and is—essentially a list of jobs. Included, in its own words, are several thousand "federal civil service leadership and support positions in the executive and legislative branches of the federal government that may be subject to noncompetitive appointment." About twelve hundred of the executive branch jobs on the list (the figure fluctuates) are filled by presidential appointment; nominations to them are confirmed by the Senate.

But as seen by the members—Principals—of the newly organized Center (later Council) for Excellence in Government, the Plum Book left much to be desired. Missing was any information about the purpose and function of those twelve hundred positions, what issues they dealt with, the environments in which they operated, or who was best qualified for them. That knowledge, these Principals felt, was vital for those at the White House who shape presidential appointments and for the appointees themselves. They thought there were others with an important need to know, such as members of the Senate and the media.

The Principals were not alone in these views. A 1983 study published by the National Academy of Public Administration (*America's Unelected Government: Appointing the President's Team*) called the Plum Book "only a starting point." It listed appointed jobs but offered no information on the responsibilities involved or "the kinds of demands their incumbents will have to satisfy." Authors John W. Macy, Bruce Adams, and J. Jackson Walker said neither the Plum Book nor the statutes that established the jobs come close to describing the "dynamic quality" of senior appointed positions.

To fill this gap, the Council in 1987 invented the Prune Book. It would focus almost entirely on the subcabinet of the executive branch, positions ranging in level from deputy secretary to assistant secretary in cabinet departments and their counterparts in independent agencies. It would describe jobs chosen for their central roles and accountability in guiding the most important work of the federal government. By developing original information about those jobs and profiling them in detail, the book would serve the goal of helping bring more qualified people into the executive branch's top political leadership. It would bring the jobs alive, make them real for appointees and appointers alike, and give all readers a grasp of what they were about. Publication of the book would coincide with the 1988 presidential election.

As for its title, those who created the idea sought to contrast the book's content with that of the Plum Book. They saw a parallel between the experience born of knowledge and exposure and the maturing process in which a plum becomes the crinkled but dependable edible we call a prune.

If the Plum Book was a list of appointed jobs, the Prune Book would emphasize the requisite knowledge and experience to perform well in them.

When it appeared in late October 1988, describing 116 positions, the first Prune Book clearly represented only an experiment. No real expectation existed that others would follow—although we did express the hope, in a foreword, that it would be "the first in a long line of many useful editions." In any case, within a few months it was clear to some of us that no successor book would ever see the kind of publicity that the 1988 volume received before and after it came out. For that, we could partly credit the presidential election itself, the first in twenty years in which an incumbent president was not running, as well as the novelty of the book's title. Media coverage of the book engaged network and cable television in this country and abroad; Washington local television stations; network and local radio nationwide; half a dozen prominent U.S., British, and Canadian news magazines; and about 125 big- and small-city newspapers, including the three best-known dailies in the country. And, if imitation really is the sincerest form of flattery, we were pleased a year later when a New Jersey organization, with our approval, published a similar work covering senior appointed positions in that state.

One result of all that was that other editions of the Prune Book followed. Two, in 1992 and 1993, addressed appointed positions in science and technology and financial management, respectively. We produced them at the request and with the sponsorship of eminent nongovernment professional groups—the Carnegie Commission on Science, Technology, and Government and the national public accounting community. Each saw the utility of helping raise the quality of appointments and performance in specific federal executive positions in these fields. Three other more generally focused books appeared in conjunction with election years 1992, 1996, and 2000.

Beginning in 1996, the scope of Prune Books began to broaden. In addition to position profiles, they considered other significant elements of the world of appointed service. One of these essays offered a soup-to-nuts examination of the appointments process and the confusing maze through which presidential appointments and nominees must (to this day) struggle. Another laid out the leadership challenges facing appointees at the many levels of their everyday responsibilities and suggested ways to meet them effectively. This year's volume, the seventh, looks at the management resources appointees can use to meet their responsibilities, functional strategies now at the center of governance, and the work of newly prominent coordinating councils for managing government.

The Prune Book was initially conceived as a presidential transition resource for White House personnel officials, the Senate, and the media. Although media coverage has never matched the level attained for the first book in 1988, it has more than adequately illuminated the objectives and product of the project. Anyway, media attention and book store sales figures matter less for a book of this kind than whether it is read and used by its primary audience: executive branch leaders including appointees, other senior managers, legislators, journalists, opinion-shapers, and teachers.

On that score, as indicated, anecdotal and other specific information suggests positive impact. For example, conversations with George H. W. Bush's director of presidential personnel and his colleagues showed that the personnel office had made extensive use of the 1988 book, especially at the outset of that administration. They consulted it as a central resource and bound photocopies of its profiles into the office's main reference document. In addition, staff members said they had desk copies of the book and used it regularly to contact former occupants of jobs, enlarge their knowledge of positions in their jurisdictions, and assess candidates. The director of presidential personnel also used the book to prioritize the importance of jobs in advance of the transition period (the Council supplied galleys to both presidential candidates in 1988, and both subsequently provided dust-jacket endorsements of the book).

Again, during the first Clinton campaign and transition in 1992–93, campaign and White House officials asked for multiple copies of all Prune volumes to date. In 1997, the Council began discussing with the Clinton White House a potential collaboration in the orientation of new and recent presidential appointees. The conversation developed partly from the 1996 Prune Book's advocacy of organized, systematic preparation of all appointees. That recommendation wasn't the only factor in the White House's later decision to develop a mechanism for orientation of senior appointed leaders in the executive branch. But it appears to have played an explicit role in raising receptivity to the idea among the president's chief of staff and others. That year saw the first of three White House–Council appointee orientation programs in 1997–99, a project subsequently strengthened by the George W. Bush administration, beginning in 2001, and boosted importantly by the Presidential Transition Act of 2000, which provided funds specifically for appointee orientation.

Over the years of the series, correspondence and oral comments show that a large number of individuals have found Prune Books helpful, whether as nominees or confirmed appointees. An early example was the transition official who used the first book to help identify potential appointees to Labor Department posts and later assumed one of the jobs himself. He also reported that the book was of "great value to the people we wanted to recruit." A current example is an official very recently in government, who said, "I think it's a good tool. It helps people understand the nature of some of the senior assignments in government and what's required to do them effectively." There have been many examples in between. Prune Books appear on the shelves of a number of college and university libraries. The Council regularly receives inquiries about the books, fills requests for copies, and distributes the books at its conferences and other events. Other publications on related subjects have listed the books in their bibliographies.

Survey

Beyond these impressions collected over time, we wanted the views of a significant number of informed, experienced practitioners. In May 2004, we surveyed the Council's members electronically as part of the research for the substantive content of the 2004 book. We added this question:

» If you have used, read, or been aware of previous editions of the Prune Book, what are your views on its value to incoming appointees? Should the Council continue publishing it? What would make it more valuable? How important are the detailed profiles of selected positions?

We posed a similar question to the people we interviewed individually for this year's book.

All of our respondents, then, were individuals who have served in senior federal jobs, most of them presidential appointees. And let's be clear: This was not an exercise in digging for favorable comment or praise. We sought objective views and, most of all, good ideas to add to our own about how to increase the books' usefulness to those they are meant to serve.

In all, about ninety people commented to us about the Prune series. A majority of them spoke directly to the question whether to continue publishing the books. In effect, they said yes, some of them emphatically. Samples: "Prune Books are wonderful—full of wisdom and humor! Continue publishing." "High value. Need to distribute it far and wide. Continue to publish." "Very valuable, keep publishing it! A copy should be distributed to every graduate of the JFK, Maxwell, and other schools of public service." A few respondents wondered if a printed book was the best way to distribute the content, but they did not question the quality or importance of the information.

Individual Position Profiles

Because of its particular focus, this edition of the book does not include the typically large number of individual position profiles. Most respondents, however, found these profiles helpful or important. A former appointee said, "Perhaps people realize [its value] more after service than before, especially if they come from far outside of government and think they know a better way of doing things without advice of the insiders. The profiles are valuable. Often appointees have focused on one element of a position and are not aware of other facets of the job."

An individual now serving in government liked the book's detailing of "a select number of positions" and "its examination of them in depth," compared with the Plum Book, "which just lists the title and pay grade." This appointee added: "To the degree that the Prune Book can expand and cover more of the positions, I think that's very helpful, particularly when it comes to things like transition or for people who may be seeking an opportunity to serve in government."

"Focus on the positions that last from administration to administration, perhaps on those that should not and those that should," one survey respondent suggested. In that respect, this veteran thought a future book should consider the function of public diplomacy in U.S. foreign policy and whether the elimination of the U.S. Information Agency five or six years ago, and its incorporation into the State Department, was a mistake. The same analysis, this former appointee said, might be applied to the disappearance of the National Economic Council and to whether the Defense Department's intelligence operations should continue. And: "I think the Prune Book should be more gutsy and take positions on what works and what doesn't and why."

Other representative comments on the value of position profiles:

» Much advice is given—hurled at—new senior appointees. The Prune Book gives a more distilled and practical view that is more helpful than most other sources. And keeping it as pithy as possible is valuable. The detailed profiles are of immense help to incoming appointees.

» The profiles are critical to gaining a broad understanding of the complexity and scope of the most important jobs in government.

> The Prune Book was the single most important and substantive publication contributing to my success as under secretary of____ and director of the White House____. . . . It is in the interests of appointees and the people they serve. It would be more valuable if all appointees read the book.

- » Not sure that detailed profiles are as valuable as short profiles with more detailed, generic advice that cuts across types of positions.
- » Over time, I think the general discussions of what faces the generic appointee may be of greater value than the position profiles. These tend to be influenced by individual incumbents and the challenges of a particular time and set of issues.
- » When you can hear the words of those who have actually been in government, or are in government, that are based on real live experience, those are even more valuable in helping individuals maximize the chances they're going to be successful, for whatever period of time they might be in their positions.
- » The Council should continue to provide decent profiles of the selected positions. They don't have to be extensive, but long enough to get a feel for what the job entails.

The Audience

Views on the question of audience size were explicit or implicit in a number of comments. "It's very good background," the former White House personnel director said. "Like one year, I think [the book] looked at all the financial management positions or the science positions. And I remember I would encourage my people, if they had a science job to fill, to go read that." Anyone interested in one of the specific jobs the books look at will find them very useful, he added. But he suggested the books might not have a significant audience beyond that.

A survey respondent agreed in part—"the challenge is that specific individuals will only be interested in a couple of positions"—but added that "reading across the variety of positions gives a feel for the breadth and challenge they entail." The books have been "critical to the principal persons to whom they are aimed," said another, "but also helped raise broader issues for the media, Congress, and others to consider."

Some respondents saw the book as an aid in pairing the right people with the right jobs. One said the position profiles "are helpful to prospective appointees both in giving some head start and in assisting some people to avoid positions they are not suited to, or conversely [to find those] where they are qualified." Another believed that "for some people who are under the illusion that they can choose their own jobs, it gives them a sense of what they might want to choose," and "it gives you a pretty good insight into how government's running at any particular four-year interval."

Finally on the issue of how many people Prune Books reach and serve, we can consider this view: "It should be of value to any incoming appointee, even if his or her job is not specifically covered, since it is filled with ideas on how to be effective. [It] should be of even greater value to those who are selecting appointees, to be sure they understand the challenges in each job and the qualifications required. I think the Council should continue to publish."

Further Comments

» At the beginning of the [George W. Bush] administration, I thought it would be helpful to understand some of the jobs better, and the book came highly recommended by a number of people who knew what they were doing in the government. So, I actually read more of it and systematically looked at it. I've seen it in the bookstores and thumbed it a couple of times in the Clinton years. . . . It's something that people talk about who are looking for government jobs and think of it as a resource.

» Great informational tool to start the organizational review process as you seek to align the available resources in a manner that will support your agenda.

» The Prune Book was invaluable to me at the beginning of the first Clinton administration. It gives potential appointees some structured way to consider possibilities in a chaotic time when there is little objective information available.

» I found it very helpful when I was looking for a job, absolutely.

Improving the Book

Some suggested improvements are evident in the comments already cited. Here are more:

» I would suggest adding some mechanism for a new appointee to contact his predecessors, perhaps by e-mail, and to interact with them on issues of concern.

» Over time, I think the general discussions of what faces the generic appointee may be of greater value than the position profiles. These tend to be influenced by individual incumbents and the challenges of a particular time and set of issues.

» The book could be improved with the addition of some case studies on what worked and what didn't work, with ideas as to why. Perhaps former appointees—or even incumbents—would be willing to write a few pages along these lines.

» An effort [should be] made to have it available to officials appointed in the later years of an administration as well as at the beginning.

One reply included a call for "more on the confirmation process, including some more practical discussions of how to approach it, and what to expect." Such a discussion "might be helpful (or sobering)." As noted earlier, the 1997 Prune Book covered this subject thoroughly, in the larger context of the presidential appointments process. So have other publications of the Council, such as the *Survivor's Guide for Presidential Nominees,* published in 2000. But real improvement in the overall appointments procedure, including Senate confirmation, continues to elude the responsible people and institutions. Producers of future Prune Books and others should therefore continue to underscore this damaging but stubborn problem and suggest solutions.

Conclusion

The Council is grateful to those who took the time and trouble to think out their perceptions of the Prune series to date and give us their views. While we take satisfaction in the net positive verdict, we take far more seriously their suggestions for improvement. It's encouraging to see words like "invaluable," "important," "useful," or "terrific." But we very much rely on the instincts and insights of people who can also spot the gaps and tell us what fine-tuning or dramatic change might be necessary.

From their ideas on improvements, two kinds emerge: content and style. For example, the books could be more helpful if they included contact information, giving appointees and nominees a quick, easy way to consult their predecessors. They could add value by offering pertinent war stories, perhaps authored by veterans who experienced them. They could take a bolder approach to certain issues and speak even more frankly on matters of personal attitude and behavior and about what works and what doesn't.

We are grateful for these suggestions, some of which the Council has already been considering. All of them will greatly help us plan a product that stays relevant and continues to serve the interests of better government. And, as stated in this book's introduction, the clear enthusiasm shown by the survey for significant numbers of individual job profiles is a strong factor to be considered in planning future Prune projects. Beyond the book itself, the Council is considering the creation of other resources for new appointees. One of these is an online site rich in useful facts, figures, and other information such as how to contact immediate predecessors. Another potential project is a series of roundtable discussions bringing together appointees with those who preceded them in their jobs and with selected people in the agencies in which they will be working.

We are under no illusion that the Prune Book series has radically altered the process by which presidents choose their senior appointees or, by itself, helped the executive branch to perform better. But sufficient indications exist that the books have given a sizable number of appointees a stronger grip on the nature of the world they work in and the particulars of their jobs, helped other stakeholders to a better understanding as well, and taken its place in the arsenal of those working for improvement.

Genuine, significant improvement, especially in government, usually advances by inches, not miles, and is normally measured in decades, not years. If it is to happen at all, many kinds of people and institutions must work constantly in the vineyards to push it ahead. Prune Books are designed, and seen by many, as a resource in that effort.

Index